# Happy Endings, New Beginnings

# Happy Endings, New Beginnings

*Navigating Postpartum Disorders*

Susan Benjamin Feingold, PsyD

New Horizon Press
Far Hills, NJ

The Edinburgh Postnatal Depression Scale reprinted with the permission of The Royal College of Psychiatrists.



Requests for permission should be addressed to:
New Horizon Press
P. O. Box 669
Far Hills, NJ 07931

Susan Benjamin Feingold, PsyD
Happy Endings, New Beginnings: Navigating Postpartum Disorders

Cover design: Robert Aulicino
Interior design: Susan Sanderson

Library of Congress Control Number: 2012941577

ISBN 13: 978-0-88282-402-4

New Horizon Press

Manufactured in the U. S. A.

17 16 15 14 13 1 2 3 4 5

*To my clients, who continue to inspire me and teach me about strength, human suffering and the will to overcome pain and choose life.*

Nothing is predestined:
The obstacles of your past
become the gateways
that lead you to
new beginnings.

*Ralph Blum*

# AUTHOR'S NOTE

This book is based on the author's research, personal experience, interviews and real life experiences. In order to protect privacy, names have been changed and identifying characteristics have been altered except for contributing experts.

For purposes of simplifying usage, the pronouns s/he and his/her are sometimes used interchangeably. The information contained herein is not meant to be a substitute for professional evaluation and therapy with mental health professionals.

# CONTENTS

# INTRODUCTION

Postpartum mood and anxiety disorders have been identified by Postpartum Support International as the most common complications of childbirth. Research has identified postpartum mood disorders as major factors affecting mother-infant attachment and healthy child development. Numerous studies reported by the National Institute of Health and others indicate that there is an association between maternal depression and many unfavorable conditions for children, such as low birth weight, behavior problems, physical complaints, learning difficulties and affective illness. Postpartum depression, a disabling mental health syndrome, also affects the relationship between new parents and is the major reason that some women are unable to find joy in becoming a mother.

## WHAT ARE POSTPARTUM EMOTIONAL DISORDERS?

Postpartum emotional disorders vary in their time of onset, severity of symptoms and duration. The mildest of the biochemically based disorders is *the blues* (though some doctors prefer to classify this transitory condition as a normal adjustment, because it's so prevalent). While less common, the more severe postpartum emotional disorders, usually lumped under the term *postpartum depression* (PPD), still affect a huge number of women—as many as 800,000 Americans and many more worldwide each year. That's roughly 20 percent of all new mothers. This statistic represents only the women who are diagnosed clinically with the illness and is probably lower than its actual occurrence. Many of my clients say they had a previous episode after the birth of an older child but didn't seek professional help at that time. Others indicate that they know friends, neighbors or siblings who suffered silently and never received treatment. Some women with the condition are too ashamed to admit their suffering openly or are afraid that their children will be taken away from them.

Melissa, a seventy-eight-year-old woman, called me following the publication of an article about postpartum depression in a well-known newspaper. She told me that she had the condition many years previously, after the birth of her twins, but didn't realize it had a name or that other women experience it, too. During that period, she had "bad thoughts" of harming her babies, although she always took good care of them and was a loving and devoted mother. For decades she kept her experience secret from everyone, even her husband of over fifty years. As a result, it became a burden that made her feel inadequate, full of self-doubt and low self-esteem. But after reading the article, she understood that she had suffered from an illness and finally felt free to tell her family about it. Her husband's response to this revelation was, "Had you let me know before, I could have been there to help you." This story is not as unusual as it sounds; women are more likely to go through this frightening and painful illness alone than to get treatment.

The silence surrounding mood and anxiety disorders has been reinforced by several fallacies. Societal myths that idealize motherhood have perpetuated the belief that maternity, being natural, is an easy transition. One particularly harmful impression is that during pregnancy and the postpartum year, women enjoy optimum mental health, as though they are encased in an emotional bubble. For many years, the general public and the medical community have accepted this idea, which has reinforced the notion that you are the only one who feels differently.

In reality, women are more at risk for depression during their childbearing years than at any other time. Authorities estimate that hundreds of thousands of women in the United States and thousands more worldwide suffer from some form of depression in their lives, with the onset peaking between twenty-five and forty-four years of age—the childbearing years. Slowly, this falsehood of protected mental health is becoming obsolete and a growing number of healthcare providers are educating, screening and identifying women who are at risk and referring them for evaluation and treatment.

I once read an op-ed letter from an obstetrician-gynecologist in Australia who maintained that women Down Under don't get postpartum depression. I responded that he was mistaken; in fact, there's an organization called the Post and Ante Natal Depression Association (PANDA) specifically devoted to supporting Australian women and families who suffer from perinatal depression. Many people attempt to deal with this illness by denying it, simplifying it or perhaps trying to feel safe or superior by thinking it happens only somewhere else or to someone else. Unfortunately, this isn't true, as PPD affects women of all races, religions, socioeconomic statuses and locales.

Another detrimental myth is the idea of the perfect mom or "supermom." This impossible goal sets up women to feel inadequate and stressed and to ignore their personal needs, leading to self-sacrifice, exhaustion and emotional and physical depletion—a state that's ripe for depression.

## WHAT IS POSTPARTUM ADJUSTMENT DISORDER?

The mildest, least severe postpartum emotional disorder is known as *postpartum adjustment disorder.* It can begin within the first three months after the birth and shows as depression, anxiety or both. In an adjustment disorder, symptoms are related to the psychosocial stressors of having a new baby rather than the hormonal and biochemical changes that accompany pregnancy and childbirth, so medication is generally not needed. Instead, psychotherapy, new mother support groups and playgroups are recommended. These adaptations help moms work on strategies for coping with and settling into their new situations and provide support from other women in the same stage of life, with whom they can share experiences and develop friendships.

## WHAT IS POSTPARTUM DEPRESSION?

*Postpartum depression* is an umbrella term for a variety of moderate to severe symptoms of depression and/or anxiety that need professional mental health identification and treatment. Despite the name, this disorder can occur without depression or low mood. Women who are experiencing significant anxiety, panic attacks and/or obsessive thoughts frequently contact pediatricians and pediatric nurses with questions and concerns, hoping for reassurance, but are not diagnosed as having postpartum depression. Some of the women may not be taken seriously, regarded as just neurotic or nervous new moms. It's important for healthcare professionals to be aware of the many ways that postpartum illness presents so they do not minimize or overlook legitimate cases but provide these women the help they need as quickly as possible.

Postpartum depression, like other emotional disorders, is identified by its cluster of symptoms, their severity and the time of onset. A woman's subjective experience of distress and the effect of her symptoms on her current level of functioning also assist in diagnosing the illness.

Any one case of postpartum depression can include symptoms from any combination of four subgroups: depression, anxiety, panic disorder and obsessive-compulsive disorder, each of which has its own different assortment of symptoms. Depression is not always a component. Don't be confused by other names you may have heard postpartum depression called, such as postpartum illness, postnatal disorder, postnatal depression (used frequently in the United Kingdom) and perinatal disorder. They mean essentially the same thing. However, postpartum blues, postpartum adjustment disorders and postpartum psychoses are distinct from postpartum depression and these terms are not interchangeable.

Although postpartum depression comes at a most difficult time and makes for a discouraging beginning as a new mom, it is not the end of the story. It can be pivotal in a woman's personal growth, enriching and changing the course of her life. In broadening your perspective, you'll see how this experience can lead to positive growth and, ultimately, a metamorphosis.

As a clinical psychologist, I specialize in the diagnosis and treatment of women with antepartum (before childbirth) and postpartum depression and anxiety disorders, as well as other reproductive-related issues, such as infertility, menopausal problems, perinatal loss, female sexual troubles and the complications that couples experience in their relationships as a result of these difficulties. I'm also an adjunct professor at Argosy University, Chicago, where I teach a graduate course in antepartum and postpartum mood disorders. I served on the executive board of directors for Depression After Delivery, a national nonprofit known affectionately as DAD that has since disbanded due to lack of funding, and was president of the organization for two years. In addition, I have been facilitating postpartum depression/anxiety support groups at a United Way agency and practicing privately in this specialty for more than nineteen years.

However, that is not how my story begins—nor what gives me a true understanding of this disorder. My interest was born out of the hardest time of my life, worse than adolescence and divorcing after twenty-six years of marriage. It resulted from my own postpartum depression.

The real story began nearly twenty years ago with the birth of my second child. I had been working as a clinical psychologist for a short time after finishing a rigorous and demanding doctoral program. Throughout adulthood, I had dreamed of becoming a clinical psychologist. Although my plans were waylaid for many years by marriage, the birth of my first child and a job as a school psychologist, I finally earned my advanced degree and took a position I loved at a large Veterans Administration medical center.

My second pregnancy had been normal until one point in the second trimester, when a nurse unexpectedly performed a Heimlich maneuver on me during a routine CPR course. Knowing I was pregnant, she announced that she was going to demonstrate where to place your hands when performing the maneuver on a pregnant woman. Unfortunately, she did more than simply indicate where the hands should go. Her impulsive act landed me in the emergency room that night. It triggered contractions and preterm labor that lasted throughout the rest of my pregnancy. As a result, I spent the next few months on bed rest.

Despite this scare, I gave birth to a healthy baby boy via normal vaginal delivery. However, within days I fell into what felt to me like a living hell (known clinically as severe anxiety and depression) that continued for the next eight months. Whenever a trauma precedes postpartum depression, it's unclear whether the condition would have surfaced without that event. My disorder started with sleep difficulties and insomnia so acute that I wasn't even sure whether I was sleeping at night. This led to extreme exhaustion coupled with obsessive thoughts and anxiety over retiring each evening, as I fretted over yet another restless night, tossing and turning while everyone else in the household, including my infant son, slumbered peacefully.

I experienced most of the same symptoms that my own clients disclose: loss of appetite, total absence of joy and motivation, extreme sadness and depression, easy and frequent crying with little provocation and obsessive thoughts about needing to sleep. As if that weren't enough, horrifying fears that the Heimlich maneuver had injured my son and that something was wrong with him—as well as absurd, distressing thoughts seemingly out of nowhere that I might abuse him—terrified me. Consequently, I dreaded being alone with my baby, in addition to feeling severely anxious and agitated.

Although this was my second child (my older one was already ten), I felt wholly incapable and inadequate as a mother. I often believed that both of my children, plus my husband and the rest of my family—in fact, the world—would be better off without me. Many new mothers also suffer from panic attacks and notions of suicide. I only had panic-like bouts and suicidal thoughts, never an actual plan to harm myself, but I was still at risk. Thankfully, my close friend from out of state came unexpectedly for a weekend visit after intuiting my desperation during one of our many phone calls. If not for her, I probably wouldn't have received the help I needed.

I went to many well-meaning therapists, from social workers to psychologists and psychiatrists. Either they didn't know how to treat postpartum depression or they gave me misinformation, such as saying the condition lasts only up to about three weeks, so I couldn't have that disorder. One psychiatrist told me my problems were caused by an unhealthy early relationship with my mother and I would have to spend months—maybe years—in psychotherapy exploring that period.

Women suffering from postpartum depression are so confused and desperate that they tend to be especially vulnerable to suggestion, believing whatever "the experts" or sometimes friends and family tell them. Because of my own foggy state of mind, for example, I accepted the doctor's conclusion that my relationship with my mother caused my depression. Though I'd never had postpartum depression—or any major depressive illness—before, even after the birth of my first child, I was willing to question my relationship with my mother. Fortunately, I soon realized that this psychiatrist didn't know what she was talking about. Even so, I repeatedly asked my husband whether I could have been depressed for years and just wasn't aware of it. He reassured me that I had never, *ever* been like this before.

Since my condition, like many cases of postpartum depression, manifested in an anxious, agitated state, I found a social worker who specialized in anxiety disorders and had a consultation with him. He was willing to listen and help me through the most difficult period of my life without over-pathologizing me or relating my current symptoms to my early years.

I believe that people need to make sense of their lives. In the midst of an experience like postpartum depression, they frequently ask, "Why did this happen to me?" In fact, it's typically one of the first questions my clients pose in our initial sessions.

The painful experience of my depression, along with my difficulty in finding a professional who could really treat it, altered my life and the course of my career. As part of my search for meaning in postpartum depression, I resolved that when I got well, I would devote myself to providing women and their families with the knowledgeable help they need in their struggles, too. This quest for meaning also fits my belief that we are each meant to follow a certain path, one in which we use our personal gifts or talents to serve humanity and thereby end up more fulfilled ourselves.

After this difficult period I changed my career path and devoted myself to treating only reproductive-related mood and anxiety disorders, becoming a specialist in postpartum depression. When I first told my friends and colleagues of my plan, which meant leaving my Veterans Administration position—a job I enjoyed and that offered advancement potential—they were not encouraging. I heard such comments as, "You can't have a practice treating only postpartum depression" and "There aren't enough women with postpartum depression to justify a full-time practice." This just made me more determined.

For approximately ten years, I treated postpartum depression exclusively. Lately, this full-time practice has grown its client base and expanded to cover other women's health, relationship and reproductive issues in response to the changing needs of my clients, some of whom had more children, suffered losses, developed fertility problems, experienced sexual or couple-relationship issues or entered menopause.

Martin Luther King once said, "Everyone has the power for greatness; not for fame, but greatness, because greatness is determined by service." Early on in becoming a psychologist, I decided that my service would be to help others with their emotional pain. Treating postpartum disorders has been a particularly meaningful way for me to follow my path and accomplish that goal.

Therapists not only help their clients get well and grow, but also they undergo growth themselves through helping clients. The women I've worked with have taught me about postpartum mood disorders in many forms. My work has allowed me to process my own experience as well as find meaning and make sense of the intense pain I endured in that first year of my son's life—a time that proved to be constructive and life-changing and that came to fill my work with significance and satisfaction. Simultaneously, it has allowed me to observe and facilitate my clients on their paths as they find meaning in their own experiences and personal growth in what lies beyond this illness.

*PART I*

# POSTPARTUM EMOTIONAL DISORDERS

# CHAPTER 1

# *Testing Truths and Falsehoods about Postpartum Depression*

There are many falsehoods about postpartum depression, the women who experience it, those who are likely to suffer from accompanying mood disorders and what helps them to recover. What ideas do you entertain? Let's test your knowledge about the illness and see more clearly the myths you hold.

On the next few pages you'll find some questions about your symptoms and feelings as well as the truths behind mistaken ideas. Then we'll look at some information, tips and strategies that can help you understand and cope with the emotional upheaval you are experiencing.

## Postpartum Quiz

1. You probably won't get postpartum depression if you haven't been clinically depressed before.

   True False

2. If you had postpartum depression before, your knowledge "prepares" you so you're unlikely to get it again.

   True False

3. “Supermoms” are not the type to get this illness.

   True False

4. Nursing your baby will protect you from postpartum depression because of the additional hormones you’re secreting.

   True False

5. The illness shows up only in the first few weeks after delivery. If you get depressed after ten months, it can’t be postpartum depression.

   True False

6. If you stop nursing suddenly, you may be at risk for postpartum depression.

   True False

7. Mothers who have postpartum depression always have trouble bonding with their babies.

   True False

8. It’s not a good idea to hear about the illness when you’re pregnant, because if you’re suggestible you’ll be more likely to get it.

   True False

9. Taking medication is the only way to get rid of postpartum depression.

   True False

10. Mothers who experience panic attacks have anxiety, not postpartum depression.

    True False

## Some Answers to Faulty Beliefs

1. You probably won't get postpartum depression if you haven't been clinically depressed before.

   **False.** However, a prior history of the disease can actually increase your risk.

2. If you had postpartum depression before, your knowledge "prepares" you so you're unlikely to get it again.

   **False.** Subsequent births increase your risk of developing postpartum depression to between 33 and 50 percent, but prevention can help reduce your chances.

3. "Supermoms" are not the type to get this illness.

   **False.** Anyone can get it. In fact, unrealistic expectations may put a new parent at greater risk.

4. Nursing your baby will protect you from postpartum depression because of the additional hormones you're secreting.

   **False.** There's no evidence of this.

5. The illness shows up only in the first few weeks after delivery. If you get depressed after ten months, it can't be postpartum depression.

   **False.** It can happen anytime in the first year but most commonly occurs in the first three to four months.

6. If you stop nursing suddenly, you may be at risk for postpartum depression.

   **True.** This can be the trigger for some women (though others feel better when they stop nursing).

7. Mothers who have postpartum depression always have trouble bonding with their babies.

   **False.** While this is true in some cases, many mothers still feel connected to their babies.

8. It's not a good idea to hear about the illness when you're pregnant, because if you're suggestible you'll be more likely to get it.

   **False.** Hearing about the disease beforehand may help you recognize symptoms and seek professional counseling sooner.

9. Taking medication is the only way to get rid of postpartum depression.

   **False.** Therapy and support groups are useful too and may be the only form of treatment needed.

10. Mothers who experience panic attacks have anxiety, not postpartum depression.

    **False.** Postpartum panic disorder is one type of postpartum depression.

The short true-false quiz you just took is a self-test of your knowledge about postpartum mood disorders. There are various standardized screening assessments and inventories that have been administered to large groups of women to make comparisons between their scores in order to diagnose postpartum depression.

The Edinburgh Postnatal Depression Scale (EPDS) is one of the most common screening tools for postpartum illness. The EPDS is a ten-item self-report questionnaire; the woman chooses the statement that best describes how she has felt in the past seven days. Each statement is rated between zero and three, with higher scores reflecting more significance for postpartum depression. Some items are reverse scored and a total score of twelve or higher is considered significant for postnatal depression.[1]

The Postpartum Depression Screening Scale (PDSS) is a thirty-five-item self-report instrument in which women read statements and then rate the sentences as *strongly agree*, *agree*, *disagree* or *strongly disagree*. In developing this scale, Cheryl Beck, DNSc, interviewed mothers who were suffering from postpartum depression in order to describe the essential structure of the illness.[2]

Many of the other common standardized instruments used to diagnose postpartum depression are not self-report scales, meaning that the screening tool is administered by a healthcare professional in a semi-structured interview format. An example of this is the Postpartum Depression Checklist (PDC), also developed by Cheryl Beck. The PDC assesses eleven symptoms ranging from lack of concentration to more serious themes such as suicidal thoughts. This test is used "to engage a mother actively in a dialogue about her experiences with these eleven symptoms."[3]

Sometimes screening tools and paper and pencil instruments can be useful, as they provide a quick way to alert healthcare professionals that a mother needs to be referred for further assessment and/or treatment. According to psychologists and authors Susan Dowd Stone and Alexis E. Menken, "Clinicians, particularly those in doctor's offices, clinics, and hospital settings, are likely to find standardized psychometric tools a simple and effective diagnostic procedure."[4]

However, there is no substitute for an in-depth diagnostic interview in which the clinician can assess the client with a thorough evaluation session. The first session usually focuses on obtaining information regarding current symptoms and a detailed mental health and prior treatment history, as well as setting up treatment goals. "Allowing the mother an opportunity to narrate her story in a semi-structured or open-ended conversation proves invaluable to diagnosis and treatment; nothing replaces the value of the face-to-face personal interview," according to Stone and Menken.[5]

# CHAPTER 2

## *The Postpartum Continuum*

It is difficult while you are experiencing the painful symptoms of postpartum depression to come to grips with the emotional disorder. However, to understand postpartum depression, you must first appreciate the significant, though typical, emotional consequences that accompany the birth of a child. Think of postpartum emotional disorders as lying along a continuum, with the often difficult but usual changes at one end and psychosis at the other; various postpartum mood and anxiety disorders and other adjustment problems fall in between.

While childbirth is normal, it's a life-changing event fraught with cascading effects that require enormous adjustment for the woman, her spouse and the couple together. Even in the best circumstances, it's accompanied by a great deal of stress and parents are often unprepared for its full impact. Many couples find it difficult to adjust to the lack of spousal attention and apparent dwindling of affection that can occur; spouses can feel neglected or unloved when their own needs take a subordinate position due to the sudden focus on the baby and this can cause resentment, disconnection and alienation between partners.

The more parents know about the postpartum period, the more control they'll have over the inevitable changes it brings—and over their lives in general. Yet birthing classes and doctor visits concentrate on pregnancy and delivery only and devote very little time to educating couples on how to handle life after the baby comes: teaching coping strategies and advising future moms and dads to modify unrealistic expectations, curb their perfectionism and maintain a sense of humor. It's no surprise that when schedules turn upside down and the infant seems to be the one controlling the grown-ups, new mothers often feel a loss of control.

Some other common effects among women at this time include a lack of physical and emotional energy while they recover from childbirth and deal with sleep deprivation, a reduction in leisure time and activities and a drop in discretionary finances, even if they return to work. (Having a baby is expensive and when the mom works outside the home, she often needs to pay for child care.) On top of that, women undergo a major transformation involving their roles and identities as they integrate the concept of motherhood with their previous sense of womanliness.

One of the most profound changes, however, is in the couple's relationship. If that was strong prior to childbirth, maintaining it may be relatively easy. But the protracted stress of a long, severe postpartum mood disorder can challenge even the most solid bond. Sometimes the effect is evident when the woman is actually ill; other times the full impact is seen only years later. Several of my clients who have come back to treatment while undergoing a separation or divorce have said that it was during the postpartum period that they and their partners first felt a loss of connection or began to detach from each other. This may happen when a spouse is non-supportive, judgmental or critical of a woman going through a postpartum emotional disorder. Resentment can build in both partners and if it's not dealt with openly and directly, it can doom the relationship.

Each of us handles change differently. We may welcome it or struggle against it. Those who adjust well to new situations and can "roll with the punches" may have an easier time when major adjustments, whether planned or inadvertent, are called for and stress arises. These differences become pronounced during the postpartum period. Many new mothers who seek treatment for adjustment problems have admitted that they had trouble managing other changes in their lives, such as leaving home for sleepaway camp or college, beginning a new job or getting married.

The birth of a baby is likely to be one of the most significant and stressful changes of all. It's understandable that women who struggle with other adjustments in life will often experience difficulty coping during this critical time as well. It may help to realize that it takes time to adjust to your new life, to assimilate the role of mother into your previous identity. Many women say they feel disoriented and alienated from themselves. "I just don't feel like myself" is a common complaint. Too often women believe they have to abandon the old "me" in order to assume this new persona called mother. A healthier approach is to incorporate the maternal aspects of your being into your own individual sense of self. There are many ways to express motherhood and each woman has to discover the way that lets her maintain her uniqueness.

In addition to these identity and psychosocial factors, there are hormonal and biological/genetic elements at play. About 80 percent of women will experience hormonally driven fluctuations in mood post-delivery (better known as the postpartum blues). These mild to moderate symptoms may include crying, irritability, anxiety, restlessness and acting "oversensitive" or "overemotional." Typically beginning around the third or fourth day after giving birth and lasting up to two weeks postpartum, the blues almost never require treatment. Some clinicians consider the blues to be the mildest of the hormonally-based postpartum emotional disorders, in that the majority of new mothers experience these mood symptoms. Mothers and fathers need to be educated about them, but parents can also be reassured that the blues should be regarded as temporary, normal mood changes associated with delivery and that they will probably subside shortly.

## COMMONLY ASKED QUESTIONS AND ANSWERS REGARDING POSTPARTUM DEPRESSION

### What is postpartum depression?

Postpartum depression is the name most commonly used for the psychiatric syndrome or disorder following childbirth that includes a variety of moderate to severe mood and anxiety symptoms that require professional mental health treatment.

The clinical symptoms can include: insomnia and sleep disturbances, lack of clarity in thinking, extreme fatigue, sad and depressed moods, lack of appetite, worrying and severe anxiety, panic attacks, obsessive thoughts, feelings of hopelessness, worthlessness and poor self-esteem, loss of pleasure and motivation in usual activities, difficulty functioning at usual level, feeling overwhelmed, inability to cope with life's demands, suicidal thoughts and not feeling like oneself.

### How common is postpartum depression?

Today, 10 to 20 percent of childbearing women experience postpartum mood disorder. This illness affects millions of women worldwide each year. The illness usually begins in the first three to four months after the birth, but can occur anytime in the first year.

### What is the cause of postpartum depression?

While the exact etiology is unknown, there is generally thought to be a link between postpartum mood disorders and the dramatic hormonal changes that occur following delivery, when estrogen and progesterone drop suddenly and drastically to levels similar to those experienced pre-pregnancy. The illness is probably the result of hormonal, biological, relationship, psychological and social factors that all converge at this time. Although the symptoms may appear the same in several women, the constellation of factors that led to their disorders may be different for each of them.

### Do all women experience the blues after having a baby? How is that different from postpartum depression?

Up to 80 percent of women experience maternity or baby blues, which is not to be confused with PPD; it is not the same thing as postpartum depression. The baby blues typically begin around the third or fourth day after delivery and can last up to two weeks postpartum. These symptoms are so common that some clinicians consider them a "normal" postpartum reaction, likely related to the drop in hormones following childbirth. The symptoms can include: weepiness, some emotional oversensitivity and instability, intermittent sadness, anxiety and irritability. The symptoms are short-lived; most women need reassurance but generally do not require treatment for baby blues.

### If a woman has had postpartum depression, is she at risk for a recurrence with a subsequent birth?

There is an increased risk of postpartum mood disorders if a woman has had a prior episode of PPD. The risk increases to between 33 and 50 percent with a subsequent pregnancy.

### Can a woman prevent PPD?

Various researchers and clinicians are working on this issue. There seem to be ways women can improve their chances of preventing a recurrence of PPD; however, there is no guarantee that it can be prevented. Some women have good results with the use of estrogen and progesterone administered immediately following delivery—although there are health risks associated with hormones at this time. (Check with a physician.) Others use psychotropic medications as a prophylactic prior to the appearance of symptoms. Some women set up postpartum prevention plans, utilizing their support networks, realistic expectations and coping strategies, and achieve good results.

### How long does PPD last?

Recovery is a process that is different for each client. The general finding is that with treatment, PPD can last between six and twelve months. Without treatment, PPD can last well beyond the first year. According to some medical sources, 25 percent of women who don't get treated will not recover. It is better to get treatment!

### How is PPD treated and what is the process of recovery from PPD?

There are three components to optimal treatment: psychotherapy, a postpartum depression support group and oftentimes medication to relieve symptoms and help change brain chemistry.

Psychotherapy for postpartum depression is most effective when it is present-focused: helping women to alleviate their symptoms, teaching them new, effective coping strategies, helping to problem-solve specific issues, providing education regarding the illness and offering support and reassurance as women adjust to new motherhood and attain emotional well-being. As symptoms begin to subside, there is an opportunity to search for meaning in the experience of postpartum illness.

### What if PPD is not treated? Can a woman get well if she doesn't get help?

There are risks in not getting treatment for PPD. It may last longer and become a chronic problem or it may get worse instead of better. Is it worth it to take this type of risk with your emotional well-being and the health of your family? PPD has a recovery rate of over 90 percent with treatment; it's worth it to get help.

### What are the effects on the child when his or her mother is depressed?

There are numerous studies reporting negative outcomes for children when mothers are depressed. The research findings suggest that maternal depression can negatively impact a child's cognitive development, can lead to emotional and behavioral problems as well as learning difficulties and can interfere with attachment and mother-infant bonding. Children are "more likely to have behavioral problems, such as sleeping and eating difficulties, temper tantrums and hyperactivity" as well as "delays in language development" if their mothers' PPD goes untreated, according to the Mayo Clinic.[1]

### What can spouses and family members do to help?

Spouses and family members can do a lot to help by providing emotional support for the mother with PPD and taking over some of the responsibilities for infant care and housekeeping duties. Families can be critical in encouraging the PPD mom to get treatment; this is one of the most important things that will help her to get well.

### What are the risk factors for PPD?

Several risk factors predispose women to postpartum depression and anxiety disorders, but a woman can develop the condition even if none of them are present:

- Previous history of antepartum or postpartum emotional disorders
- A history of significant premenstrual syndrome (PMS) and/or premenstrual dysphoric disorder (PMDD) suggests a susceptibility to being hormonally sensitive
- Symptoms of depression or severe anxiety during pregnancy
- A personal or family history of depression, anxiety disorders, PPD and/or psychiatric problems, related to childbirth or not
- Major psychosocial stressors or recent stressful life events
- Lack of a social support network
- Marital or partner relationship problems
- History of physical and/or sexual abuse
- Tendency toward perfectionism or unrealistic expectations

- A previous pregnancy loss, miscarriage or stillbirth
- Fertility treatments
- Unwanted or unplanned pregnancy
- Prior traumatic birth experience
- Perinatal loss

Many colleagues and I have treated a great number of women with postpartum depression who had traumatic birth experiences or underwent fertility treatment. Could the additional hormones in these treatments, the stress involved or a combination of the two be increasing risk for a postpartum emotional disorder?

In my own practice, I have found other factors that may increase the susceptibility to postpartum adjustment problems (the less acute disorders caused by psychosocial, not biological, conditions):

- Generally poor response to adjustments and change
- An unwillingness to accept help and support (needing to "do it all by myself")
- The need for others' approval and acceptance (sometimes known as being a "people pleaser")
- Lack of previously established mechanisms or strategies to cope with stressful situations

Another common denominator among my clients is being depleted of energy. This can follow a long and difficult labor and delivery, but it seems to be more often related to the woman's lack of self-nurturing and self-care. Despite the ease with which many women nurture others, they frequently cannot give themselves enough time or attention. This may lead to exhaustion and make a woman more vulnerable to stress and emotional difficulties following the birth of a baby. In addition, I cannot emphasize enough the importance of having supportive and loving relationships with friends, relatives and one's partner. Although some mothers experience postpartum depression despite good social and familial connections, a poor social network is a risk factor, even if you're not aware of the problem. (See chapter 6, "The Benefits of Supportive Friends" for more on this topic).

Contrary to what some people think, having postpartum depression after one birth increases—not decreases—the likelihood of having another episode following subsequent pregnancies. Although the incidence of the illness among all childbearing females is as high as 20 percent, that figure can jump to 50 percent in mothers who have experienced it previously. However, there are ways to work with at-risk moms to increase the likelihood that future incidents will be less severe or, better yet, that there will be no future occurrences.

### Where can women find help?

There are many resources for assistance in finding the right treatment team (psychotherapist, psychiatrist and support group) for you. This may include various professional organizations (APA, ACOG, etc.), as well as your own healthcare providers who might be able to help you find specialists who treat PPD.

A good place to begin is Postpartum Support International (1-800-944-4PPD). Look at their Web site (http://www.postpartum.net) to get information, find professionals in your state and locate support groups.

## GOOD NEWS ABOUT POSTPARTUM DEPRESSION

Although postpartum emotional disorders are serious illnesses, they respond relatively quickly to professional treatment (sometimes within a few weeks or months). There is a benefit in screening pregnant women, in that at-risk women can be identified early and monitored closely throughout their pregnancy. Women who begin to experience mood or anxiety symptoms can receive interventions promptly, which hastens the recovery process. Physicians, nurses, childbirth educators, lactation consultants and doulas can screen pregnant patients as a routine part of prenatal healthcare, using informal questions and/or formal assessment tools, such as the Edinburgh Postnatal Depression Scale, Postpartum Depression Screening Scale and the Postpartum Depression Predictors Inventory-Revised.

The good news is that early identification of postpartum depression equals early recovery. When the condition goes on for months and months without treatment, it may not only become worse for the mother and resistant to treatment but also have negative consequences for attachment or bonding with the baby, in the couple's relationship and within the family as a whole.

Experts say that 25 percent of the women ultimately diagnosed with postpartum depression will not get better if left untreated. This is an alarming statistic. But hopefully it will encourage you and other mothers suffering from the illness to get help.

*PART II*

# POSTPARTUM ADVICE, MYTHS AND OUR SIGNIFICANT RELATIONSHIPS

# CHAPTER 3

## *Unsolicited Advice: You're Not Doing It Right!*

For some reason, people often feel they have the right to offer unsolicited advice. They don't mean to be judgmental or opinionated, but somehow they can't seem to help themselves. We all have opinions and judgments about everyone and everything. When it comes to babies in particular, many women think they're authorities and new moms seem to be a magnet for these types of comments. It's as though they wear signs that read, "Please tell me how I'm doing as a mother" or "How do you think my baby looks?" or "Be sure to let me know if I'm doing anything wrong." People often blurt out their thoughts without stopping to filter themselves or phrase things tactfully.

Does that match your experience? Despite all the years I've worked with moms in clinical practice, I never cease to be appalled and stunned by the stories I hear about new moms who are inundated with tales of what they're doing wrong and what they should be doing instead.

It is painful for a new mother to hear the "wisdom" of experienced female "authorities" at the grocery store, at the shopping mall or walking down the street. It makes me wonder why this advice always seems to come mostly from other women and not men. I feel some women can be hard on one another, lacking in compassion.

Some of the blunt comments remind me of the nuggets that spew from young children who tell you *exactly* what is on their minds. Most of my clients say that they're literally speechless in these situations; they cannot respond at all. They rarely see any humor in the situation. More often than not, they take the comments as serious condemnation and, at the least, feel offended. Some are devastated. They may worry about it for days or weeks.

Clients often bring up these encounters in therapy sessions. They weigh the "awful" transgression they've been accused of and their culpability. It's surprising how often they believe that a rude comment actually represents "what everyone thinks" and I find it difficult to persuade them otherwise. I try to help them see the humor, but women with postpartum depression are often unable to find humor in anything, let alone their apparent shortcomings. Women who tend toward being "people pleasers" or caring what others think of them are particularly vulnerable to this type of negative feedback.

New moms tend to be self-critical perfectionists. They do not need any extra criticism from relatives and other authorities, let alone strangers. One of my tasks in their treatment is to help them to lighten up and be less self-demanding. It's a learning curve, I like to say, as in any new job where you're inexperienced. You cannot expect yourself to become an expert without a lot of time, effort and luck. We all start out not knowing what we're doing. You have to go through a process of gaining confidence and expertise.

No one gives you an instruction manual, but that's okay, because no two mothers are alike, just as no two children are the same. Every mother/child relationship is unique. Trust that you will find your way. Don't strive to be a perfect mom; perfect does not exist. Just be a good-enough mom. It's hard to sell this realistic, gentle way of thinking to my most self-punitive clients and the negative influence of harsh critics only makes it tougher. Unfortunately, I cannot protect you from nasty, fault-finding busybodies or their venomous words. I can, however, suggest you try not to take their comments to heart.

What can you do when strangers give you unwelcome recommendations? First, take a few moments to recover your composure.

After that, there are a number of things you can do within your rights as a parent:

### What to Do When You Receive Unwanted Suggestions from Strangers

- Turn around and walk away.
- Stick out your tongue and then walk away.
- Put your hands over your ears and walk away.
- Run away as quickly as possible.
- Scream at the top of your lungs.
- Laugh hysterically like a crazy person.
- Stand there and glare at the person.
- Cry and make the person feel guilty.
- Yell at the person in your loudest, scariest voice.
- Ignore the person.

You have to lighten up and see the absurdity of the situation, particularly if the unrequested advice is from a stranger. There is something wrong with anyone who comes up to a perfect stranger and tells the person what s/he thinks. It is not your job to fix this person, nor should you interpret the person's comments to mean there's something that needs fixing in you.

I'm reminded of Gayle, a client I treated who had been feeling anxious about taking her newborn out of the house by herself. Finally she got up the nerve and took her baby to the supermarket. She was waiting in the checkout line when a woman she had never met looked at the sleeping child and said, "You had better have that thing on your baby's face (a tiny birthmark) checked out." Gayle was dumbfounded, embarrassed and mortified and didn't know what to do. When she told me about the incident, I was shocked at how insensitive, nervy and outrageous this interloper was.

I recall my own experience with unsolicited comments during the period of new motherhood. It was at the time when I was pregnant with my daughter and a fellow worker asked me what we planned to name the baby; we already knew it was a girl. I felt compelled to respond that we had picked out a lovely biblical name. However, when I told the acquaintance the name, she made a face and said it was old-fashioned and sounded like an old lady's name. I was shocked at her nerve. I felt like I couldn't stop thinking about what she had said; it ruined the name for me. My husband and I chose a different name for our daughter and I never told anyone the new name we had decided on until my daughter was born and we made the announcement.

What's even more difficult than the uninvited comments from strangers are the unsolicited critiques from friends and relatives. These can be particularly difficult, because you likely have to maintain a relationship with the person. If the remarks come from a friend, you may choose to confront the person or even stop socializing with the person. But if it's someone you work with or a close relative, maybe an in-law or your own mother or sister, it could present a daily challenge. In addition, with a relative this is often not a one-time occurrence but more likely an ongoing situation, which you may have to address repeatedly.

---

### Jane's Story

*Jane, one of my clients, had an interfering, bossy mother-in-law. Jane's relationship with her husband's mom had always been friendly during Jane's five-year marriage, but she was well aware that the woman could be intrusive, meddling and, at times, downright dogmatic. When her husband, Sam, wanted to buy a home located near his parents, Jane agreed for the sake of their marriage. And the arrangement seemed to work, as long as Jane kept visits infrequent and phone calls relatively short. Other than occasional holidays, she didn't see her in-laws too often, since she worked long hours and had a busy social calendar. Her own parents lived close by, too, but they were easygoing, supportive and got along well with everyone. Jane's mother encouraged her daughter to ignore the jabs and insensitive remarks from Sam's mom. "Just laugh them off," she often said. "She doesn't mean anything by them. She just acts that way because Sam is her only son." So Jane put up with her mother-in-law's thoughtless comments about Jane's housekeeping and suggestions for how to be a better wife.*

*Although Jane found the criticism annoying, she didn't take it too seriously—until she became pregnant. Once she was expecting, her mother-in-law began to call more often and seemed to feel entitled to express her opinions more readily. She also stopped by Jane and Sam's house unexpectedly and told the couple that she was looking forward to playing a large part in the life of her first grandchild. Although Sam reassured his wife, Jane knew she was in for trouble.*

*Throughout the pregnancy, Jane's mother-in-law gave her opinions about everything, from the name of the baby to nursing, from mothers working to the use of babysitters and day care. Sam's mother often expressed her opinion that Jane should stay home with the baby instead of employing day care or babysitters.*

*Jane had been raised to always be respectful to elders and she found it difficult to stand up to her mother-in-law and express her growing resentment of these suggestions. Jane also had a hard time setting her own boundaries and asked her husband to talk to his mom for her. Sam found this annoying and hated being placed in the middle. It worried him as well; Jane was leaning on him more and more to intercede for her. Sam wanted to support his wife, but he couldn't understand why she was so sensitive to his mom's attitudes and opinions. "She's trying to be helpful. She just doesn't know how to filter what she says," he told her. "She's always been like that. Don't take it so personally." Jane's pregnancy continued in this manner, with Jane receiving a lot of unsolicited advice from her mother-in-law and then complaining about it to Sam and her own parents.*

*At thirty-one weeks of pregnancy, Jane developed preeclampsia, a dangerous complication of pregnancy that produces elevated blood pressure and hypertension. As a result, the doctors decided to deliver the baby prematurely by Cesarean section and their new daughter had to spend several weeks in the neonatal intensive care unit (NICU). Jane and Sam spent a good deal of time traveling to and from the hospital in order to be with their daughter as much as possible. The stress intensified Jane's anxiety, which made her even more irritable and angry at her mother-in-law's insensitive remarks. She found herself obsessing, sometimes late into the night, about the woman's criticisms. Jane's tolerance was reaching a limit. Even if she is family, Jane thought, she has no right to speak so harshly and make this tense situation worse.*

*Luckily the baby made significant progress in the NICU and soon was scheduled to be released from the hospital. Jane was nervous and insecure about her mothering skills, as any new mother of a baby with special medical needs would be. After she and her husband brought their baby girl home, Sam's parents phoned several times a day and stopped by unannounced to see their grandchild. One afternoon when Sam was back at work and Jane was alone with the baby, her mother-in-law dropped by for one of these impromptu visits. Suddenly, while gazing down at the infant, she blurted out, "She's so scrawny—not healthy looking at all." The insults continued: "She looks emaciated. Are you giving her enough to eat? Maybe you should stop nursing and feed her formula." As the day wore on, Jane endured a litany of concerns from her mother-in-law, ideas about what might have led up to the premature birth and inappropriate remarks about Jane's parenting.*

*By the time Sam got home that evening, Jane was angry and in tears, demanding that he call his mother and tell her she was not welcome in their home ever again. But Sam refused and told Jane she was the one who had a problem and needed to get some help. He would not cut off his parents. Jane's folks visited all the time, he said, and he never complained about that.*

*While relating the incident to me, Jane explained, "She has no ability to filter. I can't listen to any more of her suggestions, criticisms or unwanted remarks. I just don't know what to do, but I will not have her in my home again. In fact, I wish I never had to see her again." With a premature baby and the exhaustion of being a new parent, Jane's stress was already high. Now the tension and disagreements between her and Sam were mounting and this, in turn, created more stress.*

*After Jane vented her frustration over several sessions, she and I began to work on developing ways for Jane to handle the situation with her mother-in-law. Jane realized she needed to be assertive and set limits herself for the sake of her marriage. It wasn't fair to expect Sam to keep his mother in check or to ban the woman from their home.*

*In the weeks that followed, Jane worked on being more assertive and gaining confidence as a mom. When her in-laws offered suggestions, she wasn't so touchy. She stood up to them more often and learned to ignore some of what she considered inappropriate recommendations. She asked that they call before coming over to avoid disturbing the baby's nap schedule, she told them tactfully. This helped her be more prepared when they did visit. As Jane expressed herself more directly, she became less angry and irritable with her spouse and in-laws. The more self-assured she became, the more respectfully they treated her. In fact, she started to find that sometimes the "advice" was even useful and well-meaning. In the subsequent months, Jane and Sam adjusted to parenthood and the baby developed and matured, as did their own relationship.*

---

As I've pointed out, it's often the older, more experienced mothers who are sharing this unsolicited advice. Why? And why is it women, rather than men, who are giving the counsel? I don't believe that women as a group are more bossy or controlling or less sympathetic to their younger female counterparts than are men.

I have concluded that there may be a natural evolutionary or developmental tendency for older members of a society to train the younger, less experienced members. In women, that may largely entail teaching how to care for the young. After all, an innate propensity like this can be crucial for the survival of the species. In certain cultures, especially less-industrialized ones, elders are respected for assuming this vital function. Perhaps the primary role of mature members of a civilization is to impart their knowledge to the next cohort. Think about an older male hunter taking a young boy under his wing and teaching him how to stalk and kill prey. In some societies, it is the job of the older females (the mature mothers, in this scenario) to guide or impart wisdom to the younger ones in their new mothering roles. Perhaps people are hardwired to pass down traditions from one generation to the next for survival.

This theory tends to match some of the tenets advanced by renowned developmental psychoanalyst Erik Erikson in his book *Childhood and Society.* He describes eight ages of mankind, one of which he calls "generativity vs. stagnation," a period of adulthood when the primary concern is "establishing and guiding the next generation," as he wrote in his landmark text. People who don't generate themselves in the outside world, who fail to be productive, contribute to society or leave a worthwhile legacy, will feel like they're stagnating, Erikson believed. And this must extend beyond having one's own children.

Perhaps this is the motivating force to teach others, particularly those who are younger. I also wonder if this is the same drive that propels relationships where an older woman and a younger woman are friends, as a mentoring connection. So could it be that seeing a young, naive new mom brings out the inclination in mature women and mothers to take her under *their* wings, lead her in her role as mother and help her find meaning in the experience? It seems likely.

Volunteering such knowledge and guidance in the checkout line of the grocery store is inappropriate, even when it's well-intentioned. But people with poor boundaries seem to use this natural inclination in peculiar or aberrant ways at times. Extract what is valuable in the message if you can and ignore the worthless; try not to be diverted by the messenger.

When women start out as new moms, they are much like toddlers learning to walk. Older moms can coach new moms, but ultimately they have to stand up for themselves. Ultimately you, too, will find yourself in the position of guiding future generations and passing down the wisdom that you have learned to the generation of mothers who will eventually follow you.

# CHAPTER 4

## *Cultural Practices, Myths and Rituals*

Fear can make people do some crazy things and the possibility of developing postpartum depression is really scary. There are many myths and fallacies about how to avoid this condition. I'd like to dispel some of them now.

When someone says that a peculiar practice worked for her or her friends, I wonder whether the outcome was just a result of the placebo effect. This is a widespread, well-documented phenomenon in medical recovery that, according to *The Gale Encyclopedia of Medicine*, "occurs when a treatment or medication with no known therapeutic value (a placebo) is administered to a patient and the patient's symptoms improve. The patient believes and expects that the treatment is going to work, so it does." Placebos are known to be so effective that they are used routinely as a control in most well-designed drug studies. One attitude is: What harm does it do if it works? That way of thinking may be fine if the practice has no negative side effects. The problem is that some behaviors *can* be harmful. So in general, it's best to beware of odd rituals and to use common sense.

What are some of these strange behaviors that women are engaging in to stay healthy and free from mental illness? One that has come to my attention most recently is called placentophagia or the eating of one's placenta. Bizarre as it sounds, it's becoming more and more widespread in both the United States and Europe.

What's the basis for this trend and why do supporters encourage it? Postpartum depression has been linked to a fluctuation in hormone levels following childbirth and advocates of this practice say that the nutrients in the placenta can stabilize these levels. It's true that the organ is rich in nutritive substances and hormones, since its purpose is "to nourish the fetus, remove its waste, and produce hormones to sustain the pregnancy. The placenta is attached to the wall of the uterus by blood vessels that supply the fetus with oxygen and nutrition and remove waste from the fetus and transfer it to the mother," according to WebMD.[1] Proponents point out that most mammals ingest the placenta after birthing their young. (If you've ever seen a mare foal, a cow calf or watched your pet dog have a litter of pups, you'll understand the concept.)

A recognized authority on the subject, Mark Kristal, director of the behavioral neuroscience graduate program at the State University of New York at Buffalo, has studied placentophagia for years and his work has drawn the support of the National Institutes of Health, the National Institute of Mental Health and the National Science Foundation. Kristal was quoted by *USA Today* as saying, "People can believe what they want, but there's no research to substantiate claims of human benefit. The cooking process will destroy all the protein and hormones...Drying it out or freezing it would destroy other things."[2]

Some hospitals and medical centers treat the placenta as biohazardous medical waste, because it contains blood, and the U.S. Food and Drug Administration's stance is that there's a lack of "well-designed and controlled clinical studies to support approval/licensure" (though the FDA is currently looking into the practice).[3]

The Royal College of Obstetricians and Gynaecologists has indicated that this practice affords no medical benefit to humans and the organization disputes the postnatal depression theory.

Despite the medical establishment's discrediting placentophagia, women frightened and desperate enough are finding ways to engage in the practice. Sometimes they eat the placenta raw, but more often they cook it, blend it into a smoothie or encapsulate it. This last method entails dehydrating the meat, grinding it into a powder and packing it into clear gelatin capsules that resemble large vitamins. An article in the *New York* magazine called "The Placenta Cookbook" shows a photo of a soup pot on the stove with a caption that reads: "A fresh placenta simmers with ginger, lemon, and a jalapeño pepper."[4] (Yes, the picture includes what appears to be the organ.) The most entertaining and well-written article on the subject, in my opinion, is Joel Stein's piece for *Time* magazine: "Afterbirth: It's What's For Dinner."

As this practice has grown, more businesses have emerged to prepare a woman's placenta for her or to furnish her with do-it-yourself instructions. Brooklyn Placenta Services is one such outfit. Others can be found on the Internet: Placenta Benefits sells kits to encapsulate dried placenta. A person can even get training on how to do this for other women and then start her own business.

When it comes to the placenta, practices vary widely from culture to culture. In some, it's common to bury the placenta and plant a tree in that spot. In Hungary, burning a woman's placenta and placing the ashes in her husband's drink is used for birth control. Some people claim that dried placenta has long been used by traditional Chinese medicine for health benefits. Women's health writer Melissa Dahl points out in her MSNBC Web article "Placenta Pizza: Some New Moms Try Old Rituals," that in parts of Indonesia, the Czech Republic and Morocco, new mothers eat their placentas to guarantee future fertility.[5]

Unusual postpartum rituals and customs are not limited to the placenta. China and other regions of Asia have a practice known as "doing the month," which is related to Chinese medicine and the balance of yin and yang. In their belief, childbirth disturbs the balance of these forces and women are told to avoid yin foods like cold water, turnips and bamboo shoots and to eat a yang diet of things like chicken, eggs, ginger and rice wine. This may be connected to another Chinese idea: Due to blood loss during childbirth, a new mother is said to be in a "cold phase"; to counter this, she must keep her body warm, avoid foods that are raw or cold and eat only warm or hot dishes. In Japan, it is thought that in order to avoid birthmarks on a newborn, a pregnant woman must never look at fire. Jamaican women are told that drinking milk during pregnancy can cause their children to have lighter complexions and that if a woman has a longing for oranges she must eat them lest her baby develop an orange-shaped birthmark. In Mongolia, pregnant women are told to avoid touching one another to prevent the baby's gender from being changed. In Mexico, an adaptation of an ancient Aztec belief recommends that a pregnant woman carry a key or safety pin when there is an eclipse or her baby could be born with a cleft lip. Pregnancy and childbirth are associated with many other atypical customs and superstitions. For more on the subject, see http://TraditionsCustoms.com and Rebecca Tuhus-Dubrow's Slate Web article "Why Won't This New Mom Wash Her Hair?", just two of the many books and articles that explore this topic.

Are any of these practices effective? To find out, research anthropologists Dr. Gwen Stern and Dr. Laurence Kruckman conducted an analysis of anthropological literature. They concluded that many nonindustrialized cultures have lower incidences of postpartum mood disorders than what's found in more advanced, industrialized nations. Stern and Kruckman postulated that the difference was due to the effects of traditional rituals that support and care for new moms. They described five "protective social structures," as they called them, that assist new mothers:

1. These cultures recognize a distinct period when new mothers are encouraged to limit activity in order to recuperate. In colonial America, this was referred to as "lying-in." Today other regions, such as China, have a "sitting month" for this purpose.
2. Because it's assumed that a new mother is in a period of vulnerability, other women attend to her personal care. This may include ritual bathing, washing the new mom's hair, massaging her body, binding her abdomen and so on. These practices are found in Mexico and rural Guatemala and among Mayan women in the Yucatán.
3. New mothers are thought to need extra rest, so they're secluded for a specific period of time. In the Punjab region of India, for example, there is a five-day period when the mom and her baby are visited only by female relatives and the midwife.

4. In many developing countries, women are relieved of their work and household responsibilities and others pick up these tasks for them.
5. Special recognition and attention are given to new mothers in many cultures. In Punjab, there's a "stepping-out ceremony": The midwife bathes the mother and washes her hair and a Brahmin prepares a ceremonial meal. In Uganda, the Chagga mother is crowned with beads after having her head shaved; then she and her baby are presented publicly and greeted in the marketplace with song.

Another study by Stern and Kruckman compared the Latinas of Mexico with Chicanas living in Chicago and found a lower prevalence of postpartum mood disorders among women who practiced a ritual called *la cuarentena*. This custom combines many of the protective social structures I just described: The new mother gets a forty-day period of rest, is subject to certain bathing restrictions, eats specially prepared foods, is allowed to visit with only a limited number of people and gets help from female relatives in caring for her other children and performing domestic tasks.

Can we be indisputably certain, though, that such practices will prevent a woman from succumbing to a postpartum mood disorder? Despite anecdotal reports and a few studies such as those by Stern and Kruckman, I'm not convinced that the prevalence really *is* lower in traditional cultures with specific customs related to pregnancy and childbirth. It's possible that emotional disorders are simply underreported in those parts of the globe. The World Health Organization's Web site does not list unequivocal information or statistics on postpartum illness for various countries or regions. However, in an article published online by the *Bulletin of the World Health Organization* in May 2011, a team of researchers wrote that "estimates of the incidence of depression in women in developing countries vary widely, from 15–57%."[6]

This data sheds doubt on earlier claims of less maternal depression in developing countries. So if the practices and customs

I've mentioned are questionable in preventing postpartum depression, are there any strategies useful in avoiding this illness?

According to Dr. Laura Miller and Dr. Elizabeth LaRusso, the answer is yes and the list is long. In their article "Preventing Postpartum Depression" in *Psychiatric Clinics of North America*, these two medical doctors posit that certain behaviors (for example, a healthy eating pattern, strong social support and at least thirty minutes of aerobic exercise daily) are associated with optimal resilience in women. They suggest designing a postpartum depression prevention strategy "to identify optimal protective factors, and to craft an individual plan to help each patient approximate this ideal." Depending upon which of the "factors need strengthening for a given patient," they add, "preventive efforts can include antidepressant medication, cognitive-behavioral psychotherapy, interpersonal psychotherapy, strengthened social support, stress reduction and stress management, dietary improvements, exercise, sleep hygiene, breast-feeding support, and family planning." As they indicate, "evidence to date suggests promising interventions that, taken together and targeted to specific risk factors, may help reduce the risks of postpartum depression."[7]

Many of the coping strategies and interventions that I discuss in chapter 8, "Principle I: Finding Ways to Heal" will be helpful to you in prevention as well. Remember that having a balanced, healthy lifestyle is your best preventive tool. In addition, women at risk may benefit from setting up individualized strategies with their own psychotherapists to assess—and reduce—the likelihood of a postpartum mood disorder. Be proactive by replacing your fears with a practical, wholesome lifestyle and a personal prevention plan for optimum risk reduction and a positive postpartum experience.

# CHAPTER 5

## *A Supportive Guide for Spouses and Partners*

Sometimes when a woman is suffering from postpartum illness, her husband or partner feels insignificant to her healing. This is not true. Even though a mate cannot provide the professional care a woman needs, the partner has the power to contribute greatly, both positively and negatively, to a new mom's situation.

A supportive spouse can make such a difference. In *The Mother-to-Mother Postpartum Depression Support Book*, a first-hand account of women's stories, author Sandra Poulin indicates, "strong, faithful, understanding husbands were crucial to mothers recovering from postpartum depression."[1] Often, a woman struggling with postpartum depression is scared, confused and not acting like herself. Even if she's used to being confident, she may now feel insecure and need her partner to tell her that he will continue to support her and be there with her throughout the course of her illness. I have heard many previously self-assured, independent women tell me, in tears, that they believe their husbands will divorce them. Clients have revealed feeling panic-stricken when their spouses leave for work or to run errands; they fear their spouses won't return. Many have said to me, "Why would he want to be with me? I can barely stand myself."

## RENEE'S STORY

*Renee is the type of woman who is easy to like right away: Besides being bright, articulate and attractive, she's funny and engaging. She comes across as strong, self-assured and assertive, in part because of her tall stature, large frame and slightly deep, husky voice. But despite her appearance, she has difficulty speaking up for herself, even with her spouse, and tends to acquiesce to whatever he thinks or wants, fearing he will stop loving her or even leave her if she is not pleasant and compliant. She worries a lot about what others think of her and is often concerned that she'll be "politically incorrect" or offensive. Because she's constantly second-guessing others, Renee also has difficulty making decisions. We often refer to individuals like her as "people pleasers."*

*In her young adult years, Renee functioned well in a corporate setting and was quite successful, though she needed a lot of encouragement and worried incessantly that she was not doing a good enough job. After several years of work, Renee met her husband, Aidan, at a bar one night while she was out with friends. He was a handsome man who had a good sense of humor; they were immediately drawn to each other. She began dating him regularly. They saw eye to eye about so many things that they seemed to be meant for each other. He proposed and they married and began a life together that seemed "made in heaven," Renee told me. But very soon she found herself falling into what was, for her, a well-worn pattern: trying to please him, going along with whatever he wanted and rarely disagreeing.*

*As time went on, Renee felt trapped in the precedent she had established and unable to express her own opinions, disagree or make a decision that she feared her husband might not like. She thought that if she pressured him to meet her needs, even partially, she might lose him. Over the years, Renee became more and more resentful of having to hold in her emotions and more and more anxious. Yet her spouse never knew of her discontent, because Renee never verbalized her dissatisfaction. He didn't understand why she became nervous so easily and worried so much.*

*Some things exacerbated Renee's anxiety and the tension in her marriage. Due to her husband's work, the couple had to relocate from the East Coast to the Midwest, where Renee had no family or friends for support. In her old neighborhood she could count on her mother and sisters to help with household responsibilities. Now, when she needed a hand, she was reluctant to ask Aidan to pitch in.*

*Then Renee became pregnant with her first child. Since her husband had grown up with a stay-at-home mom and expected their child to be raised the same way, Renee felt obligated to quit her job. Once the baby was born, Aidan began working longer hours and was away from home a lot more, leaving Renee to spend long stretches of time alone with the infant, with no support network.*

*What had been difficult in their relationship in the past, Renee reported to me, became much worse after the baby was born. She particularly resented the fact that while her life had changed dramatically, her husband's was pretty much the same: He continued to spend most of his free time working out, playing team sports and spending time several nights a week with his large group of male friends. Plus, Renee felt it was up to her to do everything around the house and for the baby and she rarely asked her husband for help. This was the same maladaptive pattern she had fallen into while they were dating.*

*A combination of factors made Renee a prime candidate for postpartum anxiety and depression. In addition to the stress in her marriage and her lack of a good social support network, it's likely that she was biologically vulnerable; her parents had suffered from major depression, anxiety and alcoholism. Indeed, her mother cared for her father, who had been hospitalized on and off for depression throughout most of Renee's childhood. As a consequence, Renee, the oldest of three sisters, was charged with her siblings' care. All of this subjected her to certain environmental factors and a pattern that's typical in families where the parent is emotionally unavailable and one of the children becomes the surrogate caregiver. As if this weren't enough, Renee was in a run-down state physically and had ulcerative colitis, which contributed to the stress of not expressing her feelings and not being "authentic."*

*Renee's mood and anxiety symptoms began shortly after her baby son was born and worsened over the following months. Renee indicated to me that in addition to sleep difficulties, lack of appetite and bouts of anxiety, she had trouble concentrating and found herself ruminating and worrying for hours about what others thought of her. Out of desperation, she finally asked her husband for help. However, he tended to "cop an attitude," she said, which upset and angered her even more and led to further fears: that he resented her, that he was disappointed in her, that perhaps she should be able to take care of the baby and the house on her own. She felt inadequate, worthless and exhausted by the time she finally sought treatment.*

*Several months of therapy enabled Renee to open up with her spouse and become more honest—especially with herself. She became more assertive and admitted openly that she could not take care of everything on her own; she needed her husband's help. Initially he resisted. After a while, however, he adjusted to the new, more forthright Renee. And interestingly, these changes led to better communication between them and ultimately to greater intimacy. Because*

*Renee stopped holding back her feelings, she experienced less anxiety and anger as well as less stomach distress. As she became more empowered in her relationship, she started to feel more adequate as a mother and more confident in general. As her self-esteem improved, she took better care of herself and even joined a women's volleyball league, which led to new friendships and a support network.*

*With her postpartum symptoms diminished, Renee was willing to work on other long-standing issues such as her people-pleasing behavior and handling her feelings about her difficulties growing up. She now is developing close friendships and interests to pursue while staying at home raising her son. She feels good about the progress she's made personally and in her marriage. Renee's postpartum experience was the catalyst that led to these positive changes and in the end they helped her become the articulate, assertive, confident woman she now is.*

---

## SPOUSAL SUPPORT

Sometimes spouses can help just by reassuring their suffering partners that they will always be by their sides, they won't ever leave and they wish they could stay home with their wives and babies. Spouses who attend therapy sessions with their wives are sometimes dumbfounded to hear their wives admit that they imagine their partners have "exit" strategies and are on their way out of their marriages. It is important to eliminate this concern and reassure a new mom. This alone could change the course of a woman's healing from postpartum depression.

Another way a partner can help a spouse get better is by encouraging her to take time for self-nurture and self-care. She may resist, because some women with postpartum depression feel undeserving and become harsh and self-punitive. Some of my clients admit that they won't buy themselves anything, as they feel worthless and insignificant. "Whether you feel justified or not," I tell these clients, "take time for yourself and the irrational guilt will dissipate."

Sometimes the obstacle is the woman's own mother—in particular, one who acted like a martyr and inculcated her daughter with a similar mind-set. Such a parent may not be the best example of good self-care. She might unintentionally reinforce the erroneous belief that a new mom should be self-sacrificing and that it would be selfish for a new mom to take time away from the baby for herself. You can be the voice of reason here, letting your wife know that looking after her own needs is imperative to recovery. Remind her that if she had another illness, such as mononucleosis, she wouldn't ignore it. Not handling her symptoms and needs could end up delaying her recovery and lengthening the duration of the condition.

In the case of postpartum depression, a woman will slow her recuperation significantly if she ignores her physical and emotional needs. Tell your wife to listen to her body. A new mom needs to take care of herself so she has the energy to handle all her new responsibilities.

This advice extends to you, the spouse or partner, too. A new baby needs much care and attention. But so can coping with your wife's postpartum disorder. You need to practice good self-care to replenish your own energy, otherwise you could become run-down and risk physical or emotional illness yourself. A study by mental health researcher Dr. Janice H. Goodman found that 24 to 50 percent of men had symptoms of depression if their partners had postpartum depression.[2] No one is immune to depression. If you are struggling with a mental or physical health problem, you won't be much good to your partner.

Additionally, try to take time out to be a couple. In order to be a healthy family, it's vital that you maintain this connection. Psychology professor and renowned marital researcher Dr. John Gottman and his colleagues Alyson Shapiro and Sybil Carrére cite 67 percent of couples find marital satisfaction plunges after having a baby.[3] The demands, exhaustion and various other stressors can place a burden on the stability of the dyad. Investing in your relationship is essential; it's an area you can't afford to neglect.

There are many valuable ways that you can play a major role in your partner's healing. To get you started, I've included two short lists that will pay off with huge dividends—things you can *do* to help your spouse get better and things you can *say*.

### Things Spouses Can *Do* to Help Postpartum Moms

1. Get up with the baby or share the nighttime duties.
2. Encourage her to go to therapy sessions and be willing to go with her if she and the therapist are willing. (This will let you know what's happening and may give you insight into how you can help.)
3. Encourage her to take her medication and follow her doctor's recommendations.
4. Suggest that she get out, alone or with friends, for some fun and relaxation.
5. Encourage her to telephone, text or e-mail her friends and family. (Some moms isolate themselves, which can worsen their depression.)
6. Plan a couple's night for just the two of you to reconnect. (Make the babysitting arrangements yourself.)
7. Suggest that she take a nap during the day when the baby is sleeping or perhaps when you come home from work.
8. Take over the housekeeping duties or hire a cleaning service to relieve some of the pressure.
9. Help with the grocery shopping, cooking, laundry and other household chores until she is able to manage more of these tasks. Be flexible and suggest, perhaps, relying more on take-out food, soup and sandwiches, healthy frozen foods and the like.
10. Encourage her to join a support group and/or playgroup so she can connect with other new moms, whether or not they have postpartum depression.

### Things Spouses Can *Say* to Help Postpartum Moms

1. "I'm with you all the way. We will get through this together." (And mean what you say!)
2. "You are an amazing mother and wife and I love you."
3. "I know this is very difficult, but I believe in you. I know you will get through this and overcome this illness."
4. "You don't have to be a perfect mom. No one is. Just be a 'good enough' mom."
5. "I know you would be here for me and I want to be here to help you through this. I'm with you 100 percent."
6. "You are so important to me, our baby and our family. Don't forget that. We're all here rooting for you."
7. "You are doing better each day. Look at the progress you've made since this started." (Say this only if she really is making progress.)
8. "How can I help? What can I do to make this better?"
9. "You are so strong; I know you will get back to yourself. Just keep working on getting better for yourself and our family."
10. "It's one day at a time. Take small steps until you are well again."

Next I share and discuss the stories of couples who have dealt with PPD. These illustrate the difference a partner's support and involvement can make in a woman's recovery. Hopefully, they will help you see how quickly things can go wrong without your assistance or how stabilizing a force you can be.

---

#### EMILY'S STORY

*I recently received an e-mail from Emily, who was looking for a referral to a good lawyer. Several years earlier, after the birth of her son, she had developed severe postpartum depression, attempted suicide and was hospitalized. The baby was only a few weeks old. During her hospital stay, Emily was put on a course of medication that jump-started her road to recovery. Nonetheless, shortly after she was discharged from the hospital, her husband told her that he was filing for divorce and sole custody of their son. Emily was devastated and the news likely lengthened her already painful recovery as she had to deal with multiple losses—her marriage, her family and, worst of all, her custody and parental rights.*

*Over time and with specialized help and the support of the rest of her family, Emily made a complete recovery; she even returned to college and began a professional career. However, the postpartum illness left such a black mark against her that the child's father was awarded the care of their son. Emily went back to court many times, but the judge ruled in favor of her ex-husband, who allows her only restricted contact with their child, despite the fact that she has never posed a threat to the boy.*

*Emily is heartbroken and feels helpless to combat the stigma of postpartum illness within the legal system. Her son is now school-aged and she desperately wants to spend more time with him and build a relationship. Although she has a well-respected career in an important field, her illness has had an unfortunate outcome in terms of her personal life. What's more, her son—and likely her ex-husband—are suffering from the consequences, too.*

---

### June's Story

*June was a client who had been referred to me following her discharge from a local hospital. She had undergone treatment for postpartum depression, panic attacks and anxiety, which began just a few weeks after the delivery of her son. June and her husband had moved to the area only recently and had few friends or family nearby for support. The couple had been married for several years and they both wanted and planned to have a child and a family. Yet the difficulties that followed the birth of their son caught them off guard.*

*Shortly after returning home after the birth of her son, June started to feel anxious and panicky when she first awoke in the morning, but she didn't want to worry her husband about it. He had to return to work almost immediately after the birth, because he had not been with his present employer long enough to qualify for benefits under the Family and Medical Leave Act. His job was demanding, requiring long hours and frequent travel. June tried to be brave but felt overwhelmed at being alone with their newborn for so many hours at a stretch. Though she had dreamt of this "blessed event" for years, she started to doubt whether it had been the right thing to do.*

*At one point her husband was scheduled to leave for a weeklong business trip. As his departure day approached, she became more and more concerned about her ability to care for the baby all day and night without any relief, help or adult interaction. The day before her husband was supposed to leave, June was overcome with racing thoughts, feelings of dread and palpitations she could not control. Breaking out in a sweat and feeling faint, she worried, What if I pass out when I'm alone with the baby and drop him? What if I pass out for days and the baby is crying and hungry and there's no one to help him? These frightening thoughts only worsened her symptoms. With trepidation, she called and asked her husband to come home from work and take her to the hospital. He did so and soon cancelled his trip.*

*Over the ensuing weeks, June's husband tried to help out as much as he could while handling the demands of his job. A few weeks after her crisis, while still struggling to get better, June phoned me to see if it would be all right for her husband to come to her next appointment. "Of course," I assured her. (I had suggested earlier that they have a couple's session, which is part of my normal practice routine.) He had been concerned about her and wanted to meet me, understand what the treatment plan entailed and learn how he might facilitate her recovery.*

*During the session, he admitted how worried he'd been and that he had spoken to his boss and the human resources department about possibly taking a leave of absence (if need be, without pay). June's health and his family were his first priorities, he asserted, saying, "A job can be replaced; my wife and family can't."*

*He did end up taking off several weeks from work—and luckily did not lose his job. The time he spent at home gave all three of them an opportunity to bond as a family. June continued her treatment and began to show significant improvement. Her husband's commitment and willingness to stand by her was a great benefit, not only to her health but also to the couple and family as a whole, because it brought them all closer together.*

---

When you compare Emily's and June's scenarios, you can see clearly the role that a spouse or partner plays. In Emily's, her husband exacerbated the situation and was a further drain on Emily's mental health. In June's, her husband's dedication and care contributed to a positive outcome for everyone involved.

One important way that you can participate in your partner's postpartum experience is to educate yourself through resources that address your role in the family equation and the ways that you can help yourself and your spouse overcome this condition. Fortunately, in the past few years mental health professionals have begun to acknowledge how essential the spouse is to a mom's return to health. We're seeing more books and articles that focus on educating and advising women's partners. In *The Postpartum Husband: Practical Solutions for Living with Postpartum Depression*, clinical social worker and author Karen Kleiman provides a basic primer on postpartum illness and her own simple, straightforward suggestions, addressing such topics as coping and the feelings that you, the spouse, may have. Another of Kleiman's books, *This Isn't What I Expected,* co-authored by Dr. Valerie Raskin, devotes an illustrative chapter to the effect that postpartum illness can have on the marital relationship.

Online resources also can be of great help in furthering your understanding and are readily available. The Postpartum Support International Web site (http://postpartum.net) includes a valuable Friends & Family section. There you'll find links to a variety of helpful pages: Resources for Fathers, Tips for Postpartum Partners and an interview with country singer Wade Bowen, who shares what he went through when his wife was struggling with postpartum depression. The PSI site also provides a Chat with an Expert feature, where you can call in to free, live phone sessions and discuss topics such as symptoms, resources and perinatal mood disorders with a PSI expert.

Another good Web site is http://PostpartumDads.org, where you'll find general information, recommendations, "mistakes" partners often make and numerous personal accounts, plus so much more. As Postpartum Support International puts it, "Pregnancy and postpartum mental health is a family issue: Dads and other helpers need support, information, and connection too."

# CHAPTER 6

## *The Benefits of Supportive Friends*

If you are struggling with postpartum depression, the last thing you may want to do is to call friends you've been avoiding for a variety of "very good" reasons. Reasons such as: You just don't have the energy. You don't have the time. You never returned their calls and you feel embarrassed to call them now. You never sent them thank-you cards for their gifts. You are ashamed of feeling depressed and anxious and don't want to admit it to anyone. You think they will judge you. You think they won't understand. You think they will feel sorry for you or maybe express smug self-satisfaction that they are better mothers than you are.

These justifications may seem like very good reasons, but actually they're just a bunch of excuses for withdrawing socially and avoiding people. A woman with postpartum illness can be a lot like a turtle confronted by some unknown, feared object or animal: She hides by pulling her head back into her shell for safety. My clients do this in a variety of ways, like taking to their beds, not answering the phone, steering clear of visitors who may drop by and, in the most extreme cases, pulling down the blinds and refusing to leave their homes.

Early in my career as a psychologist, I worked in a Veterans Administration hospital. Avoidance was a pattern I often observed among clients with post-traumatic stress disorder; when some trigger aroused uncomfortable memories, withdrawing made these people feel safe, as though they were hiding in a bunker. Even when we just feel unhappy or down in the dumps, not necessarily clinically depressed, there's an inclination to avoid people.

In their book *Life Will Never Be the Same: The Real Mom's Postpartum Survival Guide*, psychologists Ann Dunnewold and Diane Sanford state, "whether you know and talk often with other people who have babies can make a big difference in your postpartum life. Research has shown that new parents who talk regularly with a person who understands their trials and joys have an easier adjustment than do new parents without such friends."[1] You may not feel like connecting with your friends and family, but I've *never* found this isolation to help anyone going through a postpartum illness. On the other hand, I have found that social avoidance can further the downward spiral of depression and significantly deepen a woman's sense of loneliness and alienation. That is the last thing that you need right now, which is why it's so important to connect with others.

## THE IMPORTANCE OF SOCIAL CONNECTION

There is a wealth of information on the recognized health benefits of social support. It increases physical and emotional well-being and promotes longevity. Two epidemiologists, Lisa Berkman, PhD, and S. Leonard Syme, PhD, did a nine-year follow-up study of nearly seven thousand adults to assess social support and its effect on mortality. The findings of Berkman, currently director of the Harvard Center for Population and Development Studies, and Syme, now professor emeritus of epidemiology and community health at the University of California Berkeley School of Public Health, have significantly affected our knowledge of the way social environment shapes health. The pair found that "the most socially isolated people with the fewest social ties to others were at the highest risk of mortality. This finding persisted even when [Berkman and Syme] adjusted for the health status of the respondents at the beginning of the study, as well as certain risky behaviors such as smoking and obesity, physical activity or the lack of it, and use of health services."[2]

Another frequently cited long-term study was conducted in Tecumseh, Michigan, over a ten-year period. Almost three thousand adults were evaluated physically (in thorough medical examinations to rule out any existing illnesses that might cause isolation) and psychologically (through tests to rate their personal relationships). The results, summarized in the book *Mind/Body Health: The Effects of Attitudes, Emotions, and Relationships*, co-written by Dr. Keith Karren, Brent Hafen, Kathryn Frandsen and Dr. N. Lee Smith, showed that subjects who had the strongest social ties and were the most socially involved had the best health, while people who were the most socially isolated had four times the mortality rate of the other group.

This convincing evidence has been corroborated by research in countries around the globe. Several studies have found that people in Japan live longer than people in the United States despite other risk factors, such as a greater incidence of smoking and high blood pressure, more stress and increased exposure to pollution and crowding. Dr. Ken Pelletier, clinical professor at the University of California School of medicine San Francisco, believes that this is due to the Japanese emphasis on human companionship and community, two of the most critical factors for wellness. In another study, Syme and a team of scientists looked at twelve thousand Japanese men in depth and found, perhaps surprisingly, that the lowest rates of mortality and heart disease were among a group of subjects who had emigrated to San Francisco. That would seem to conflict with Pelletier's research, but Syme concluded that the men in California had formed the closest social networks, family connections and friendships, thus reconfirming the value of social support.

In his article "Family Ties: The Real Reason People Are Living Longer," published in *The Sciences,* a journal of the New York Academy of Sciences, physician and epidemiologist Dr. Leonard Sagan concluded that the difference in life expectancy and healthcare support between America and some other nations lies in the decreasing level of family support among Americans. He advocated for creating more social support and involvement with other people. But have we changed much in the intervening quarter century?

"We are wired to connect," writes Daniel Goleman, PhD, psychologist and behavioral-science writer for *The New York Times.* This is the most fundamental revelation of social neuroscience, he writes in his book *Social Intelligence: The New Science of Human Relationships,* adding that this "link is a double-edged sword: nourishing relationships have a beneficial impact on our health, while toxic ones can act like slow poison in our bodies." Goleman describes the workings of "the social brain," as he calls it, and the way that neural circuitry operates in human relationships. His inference: We must behave wisely as we interact with those around us, because we all affect one another, not only in the most overt ways but also through the neurological consequences our actions have on the brain.[3] It's a fascinating book and I recommend you read it when you feel like you're able to focus on something scholarly. Until then, foster your relationships and build up your support network!

## BENEFITS TO HEALTH

More than 45,000 books and articles, in whole or in part, have been published about the connection between social support and health, including mental health, in disciplines ranging from medicine and psychology to social work, nursing and public health. This correlation has been a focus of study in psychosocial epidemiology for longer than twenty-five years. As Bert Uchino, PhD, wrote in his book *Social Support and Physical Health: Understanding the Health Consequences of Relationships,* "the strongest evidence that social support is related to health or disease comes from studies of large populations demonstrating that social support or social networks are protective against all-cause mortality; it also appears that social support is negatively associated with cardiovascular death and that it protects against recurrent events and death among persons diagnosed with disease."[4] In a review of eighty-one studies in the *Psychological Bulletin*, Uchino, a professor of health psychology at the University of Utah, along with John Cacioppo, PhD, at the

University of Chicago, and Janice Kiecolt-Glaser, PhD, at Ohio State University, found that in addition to beneficial effects on the cardiovascular, endocrine and immune systems, social relationships serve "important social, psychological and behavioral functions across the lifespan."[5]

Women in particular seem to thrive and develop psychologically within the context of interpersonal relationships. In other words, connections are vitally important to women. In fact, several developmental theorists such as Jean Baker Miller, in her book *Toward a New Psychology of Women,* and Carol Gilligan, who wrote *In a Different Voice: Psychological Theory and Women's Development*, have questioned some of the previous models of separation and independence, which are based on male development and have labeled women as immature or deficient. Miller and Gilligan suggest instead that for women, autonomy is relational and interdependent. In the influential book *Women's Growth in Connection*, a team of female researchers including Miller state that for women, attachment and relationships are essential, as they conceptualize an innovative model valuing the importance of empathic relating "at the heart of this new understanding of women."[6]

## THE VALUE OF HAVING GOOD FRIENDS

These findings illustrate how important it is to nurture your friendships and family relationships even if you have a spouse or partner for support. Friends, in particular, appear to have a special health value: Several studies have shown their benefit in alleviating the negative effects of life's pressures and providing a sort of buffer against stress. They also can relieve loneliness, which has been demonstrated to have a significant, harmful impact on the functioning of the immune system and on longevity. Psychologist James Lynch, PhD, of the University of Maryland, has been a leading researcher on the health implications of loneliness and the contributing effect of social isolation on heart disease. According to an interdisciplinary team of researchers at the University of Michigan who studied

2,754 men and women, loneliness presented a substantial health risk and was inversely related to longevity.[7]

Now that we have discussed some of the research supporting the health benefits of friendship, I'd like to turn to a few "softer" ideas by author and psychologist Judith Viorst, who states in a *Redbook* magazine essay, "Women are friends, I once would have said, when they totally love and support and trust each other, and bare to each other the secrets of their soul, and run—no questions asked—to help each other, and tell harsh truths to each other (no, you cannot wear that dress unless you lose ten pounds first) when harsh truths must be told."[8]

But Viorst is quick to point out that although the bosom buddy is a wonderful companion indeed, she realizes that friendships actually came in a host of varieties, each conducted at a different level of intensity and serving a different function. She writes about the convenience friend, like the neighbor or acquaintance with whom you exchange pleasant conversation; the special-interest friend, like someone from your book club or writing group, with whom you share an activity or interest; the historical friend, with whom you have maintained a relationship over the years because you knew each other "back when." She describes, too, the crossroads friend, like your college roommate, with whom you shared a crucial, now-past time of life; the cross-generational friend, who may be like a mother to you, bestowing wisdom from her many years (while you may be like a daughter to her, offering a fresh perspective). And then there is the close friend, whom you confide in and talk with most often; this friend is the "gem" who is the most important to us, Viorst says.

## WHY OUR GOOD FRIENDS ARE IMPORTANT TO US

This started me thinking about personal reasons for valuing friendship (whether you are in a committed relationship or not) and why we are drawn to the subject of friends: to read books and listen to songs and watch television shows about friends.

Why do we love reality TV programs and sitcoms featuring groups of friends, like *How I Met Your Mother* and *New Girl*? We seem to get vicarious satisfaction out of seeing people connect with their best buds—being privy to the intimate conversations, the mutual support, the empathy over life's travails—even if they're fictional. We love to turn to our friends and know they are there for us, to celebrate our successes and good times and to help hold us up when we are struggling with difficulties. We're envious of people who have close circles of friends. We fantasize about getting together with pals at posh restaurants for drinks and conversation. We harbor visions of hanging out and counseling each other through our latest relationship troubles. Long after these types of series have aired their last episodes, the shows continue to be popular as rentals, reruns and boxed DVD sets.

*People* and other popular magazines capitalize on girlfriends helping one another when their relationships fail (Jennifer Aniston was comforted and shielded from the paparazzi by her girlfriend Courteney Cox when she and Brad Pitt broke up). Look around and you will notice women chatting together at the gym, in cafés and while walking in the neighborhood. Our close girlfriends give us energy and are our biggest fans. When we struggle with life's challenges, they are there to support us, encourage us and cheer us on.

To find out what other women thought about the importance of good friends, I conducted an informal survey on my blog (http://post-postpartumdepressionblog.com) and social networking sites. I asked: Why do we need to maintain the connection with our girlfriends? Hopefully the responses I've included will encourage you even more to reach out and connect with your friends, not only during good times but especially when confronting stress and challenges in your life.

## Why You Need Your Good Friends/Girlfriends

- Close friends are people you can confide in; they listen and validate you.
- They give you another perspective on your problems and help you find solutions you can't see on your own.

- They listen to you talk about your relationship. You can vent and get advice.
- No matter how close you may be with your partner, men and women don't always enjoy the same activities. There are "girlie" things you can share only with your female friends: shopping, romantic chick flicks, mani-pedis.
- She's someone you never have to impress. You can just be yourself, with no makeup at all.
- She's someone you can be silly and laugh with.
- She's someone who takes away your loneliness by connecting and talking with you.
- Good friends help to make everything better.
- We're pack animals—like dogs, only with more fashion sense.
- It's evolution: Men hunted and gathered; women birthed and nurtured. Safety was in numbers. Those traits got passed on. Now they're genetic.
- It's someone to call when the best things happen and you want to celebrate; someone to call when the worst things happen and you need to cry with someone who makes you feel safe.
- As people, we are a social breed. Good friends share in our joys and sorrows. They offer a different point of view and support when things are challenging.
- I have found that someone who *is* a good friend *has* good friends.
- We have many acquaintances but few actual friends.
- Good friends are those who are always there when you need them, in good times and bad.
- You can count on friends to tell you the truth and to be on your side; they say the right things at the right time.
- A friend is somebody whom I care about and enjoy sharing my life with.
- A friend is somebody who is real with me and I can be the same with her.

- With friends, there is a ready and voluntary exchange through tears and laughter, anger and frustration and all of the other emotions that human beings have.
- You can let all your defenses down with a good friend and feel totally relaxed and safe. You don't have to put on a brave face.
- Who else is going to tell you if your butt looks big in your clothes? Who else will be around through all your good and bad times?
- No one gives you more emotional support than your best friends.
- Men don't have the same wiring, empathy or understanding as your girlfriends; they don't feel the same way that women feel.
- Good friends are on the same wavelength; we've walked in the same shoes.
- Good friends have certain ways of communicating.
- Men wear tool belts to fix things, while as women we share our emotions; we don't have to fix things.
- When depressed, we need someone to take our hand and pull us through—to make us smile and laugh, even through our tears.
- That's what I always wished for: someone to pull me out of the dark hole of fear and sadness.
- She's someone to hold your hand when you need it, to give a hug, to give words of encouragement.
- You know someone really cares about you, so you don't feel alone.
- Women friends make me feel seen and heard, supported and loved, pretty much immediately.
- I feel almost no agenda with my women friends. They are there for me and I am there for them—because we want to, with no specific goal. Well, mostly for fun or to reflect.
- I feel comfortable with my women friends. I feel held, cared for, understood.

- Most of them make me laugh—a deep, healthy, primitive laugh.
- Friends give us hope for a better day ahead, even if it's five minutes at a time.
- There's a special bond between women. It's instinct for us and perhaps we carry that nurturing as mothers from our children into our relationships.
- A good girlfriend is the one you share experiences, future plans, worries and laughs with. Good girlfriends should keep you happy and balanced and make life a whole lot nicer. I am very lucky to have true, good friends.
- We need good girlfriends for fun, support and female wisdom. I have female friends who are of so many ages; I gather a lot of strength from them. I would be lost without my girlfriends. I can't imagine being with only a man all the time!

A few women responded with lengthier ideas:

- I love connecting with my friends and sharing stories about our kids, husbands, mothers-in-law, jobs, etc.... I always walk away having received either good advice or a new perspective. With my closest friends, I feel like we connect on a soul level. I also feel like I want the best for them and they want the best for me.
- When we were young, our friends were the ones we played with and as we got a little older, they were the ones we hung out with. Now friends are people I like to bounce issues off of. My friends will give me an honest opinion or just listen to me vent. Friends can commiserate together and not judge. We share about our families, kids, grandkids, aging parents.
- Just when I think to myself, "That's it; I have totally lost it," I talk to one of my close friends and I realize I am not the only one out there who feels this way. I'm totally normal. There is an understanding that girlfriends have for each other that a male friend can't provide 100 percent. We just

"get" each other's insecurities, sense of humor, off-the-wall perspectives, body image (and bodily function) issues, etc. …It keeps us sane to have someone who can relate!

Serendipitously, I had evening plans around this same time with long-time friends from a mother-baby support group that dates back to the birth of my daughter, more than twenty-nine years ago. Six of us still get together several times a year for dinner and a night of reminiscing. We have supported one another and kept in touch all this time, through various life stages and transitions: having babies, going through the school-age years, dealing with adolescents, coping with children leaving for college and facing the empty-nest syndrome, not to mention divorce, some new relationships (our children's as well as our own) and even marriages! Here are the responses my friends gave:

- The connection that women feel with women is essential; it's a different connection than with a partner.
- Women understand what you're going through.
- Women like other women to talk with. Women "get" women better. Women understand each other better. Though my husband tries, he still doesn't get me, even after so many years.
- The importance of friends never diminishes. My eighty-eight-year-old mom recently suffered a minor heart attack; after she was released from the hospital, she arranged to see her friends. She went right to the beauty salon, as she wanted to look nice when she saw them.
- I really love my girlfriends, because they are amazingly interesting people who have great insights into life! Plus, they make me laugh.

Spending time with your friends will aid your recovery, provide you with emotional support and help you reconnect with an earlier, healthier you. If there's no one you can call a good friend, this is the time to start establishing some relationships. You may be thinking this is easier said than done. But it's a challenge well worth it in the long run. Some suggestions for how to connect with other women are: joining a support group or a children's play group, taking a class or becoming a member of a special-interest club. Be creative; there are many ways to meet others and build friendships, but it all starts with your intention. Having the desired goal is the beginning. Then make a plan to accomplish that goal.

**Consider what activities interest you:**

- Are you interested in reading? What type of literature? Fiction, poetry, drama, historical narratives, inspirational books, self-help books? Consider joining a book club or a group at your public library or attend some author readings and book signings.
- Are you interested in foreign languages? Sign up for classes at a language institute or your local community college.
- Are you interested in exercise? Join a gym, take a yoga class, sign up to run a marathon (you'll train with others in a group and meet people with a common cause).
- Are you a music or art aficionado? Take a class at a fine arts center, nearby college or museum. Join a group that attends live performances or visits galleries and exhibitions.
- Are you a film enthusiast? Subscribe to a movie group such as Talk Cinema, an organization based in several major cities—and some smaller ones—that lets members enjoy sneak previews and then discuss the movies with film critics. Meet and chat with fellow fans during intermission.

You might also consider joining a new mom's group. This is a great way to connect to other new mothers in your area and it may result in your forming new relationships, perhaps leading to some good friends. Also, see if any playgroups are forming in or around your community. Word of mouth works really well: Tell everyone you know—your Lamaze teacher, your neighbors—that you're looking for such a group. In my area, one woman started connecting women for playgroups and eventually turned her services into a nonprofit business.

You can also meet other mothers who have interests similar to yours at support groups that focus on particular issues. Some examples: For breast-feeding mothers, look into groups such as Le Leche League International (http://www.llli.org). For mothers who have experienced the loss of a child, consider grief support groups like the Compassionate Friends (http://www.compassionatefriends.org). For moms who have twins or triplets (or more!), try contacting the National Organization of Mothers of Twins Clubs, (http://nomotc.org) to find a local chapter. Moms who have children kindergarten age or younger, even newborn, should consider joining a chapter of Mothers of Preschoolers (http://www.mops.org), an organization that has more than 3,900 groups across the United States and in thirty-five other countries, all "helping moms to develop friendships."

There are so many ways to meet others. Numerous supportive resources are available through your local library, park district, social service agencies and religious community, whether you worship at a church, synagogue or mosque (even if you are not a member, they may be open to having you attend a group). Meetup (http://www.meetup.com) is a network that connects locals with similar interests and touts more than two thousand local groups and nine million monthly visitors. It's sure to offer something you'll enjoy sharing with others. Just start to make the effort and before long you will have some new friends.

## THE BENEFITS OF JOINING A POSTPARTUM SUPPORT GROUP

"A support group," as Joyce Venis and Suzanne McCloskey write in *Postpartum Depression Demystified,* "is a group of people all sharing a certain problem or concern who meet to discuss how they are dealing with it in a nurturing environment. Many women feel like they're alone in dealing with the stresses of being a new mother. What support groups provide more than anything else is the opportunity to link up and feel a connection with other mothers."[9]

Participation in a postpartum support group can be a great addition to therapy. It reminds women going through this type of depression and anxiety that they are not alone. In most cases, it's a wonderfully supportive atmosphere in which women are encouraged to speak openly and honestly about what they're experiencing, something you may be reluctant to do in other surroundings. A good group will make you feel safe and comfortable communicating directly with fellow sufferers, who in turn will lend you their understanding and encouragement.

The facilitator of a postpartum support group may be a professional mental health provider or a layperson who is a survivor of this illness. I have led postpartum anxiety/depression support groups for almost fifteen years. I've observed the benefits firsthand and I encourage you to seek a group. Since these groups allow women to discuss their most intimate fears and concerns without being criticized or judged, attendees often end up close friends.

Each group has its own individual "flavor," which may be a function of the leader, the members and/or the atmosphere where the meetings are held. You may feel uncomfortable at first and decide that this group or the whole idea of joining a support group is not right for you. While it's important that you feel safe enough to share openly, remember that the very act of disclosing your personal story to a group of strangers can make you feel ill at ease in the beginning. Please try attending several meetings. If this awkwardness does not dissipate after a few more sessions, consider that it might not be the right group for you. But don't despair; just find a different support group to join.

Taking part in a support group can provide you with a wonderful coping strategy that helps you connect, form healthy attachments to other new moms and gain support in between therapy appointments. I caution, though, that it is not a replacement for individual psychotherapy but, rather, an additional tool or supplement to treatment. As Karen Kleiman, MSW, and Valerie Raskin, MD, put it so clearly in their book *This Isn't What I Expected: Overcoming Postpartum Depression,* "often, a support group is most effective when used as an adjunct to individual therapy, or for follow-up after therapy."[10]

## HOW TO FIND A POSTPARTUM SUPPORT GROUP

There are many ways to find a local support group, although the most direct way is to contact Postpartum Support International at 800-944-4PPD or http://postpartum.net. The Web site offers a wealth of information and you can click on various links to read facts, find help or become a member. To locate a support group, click on the *Get Help* menu choice and then choose Find Local Help (a button on the right side of the page). The local help link takes you to an interactive map and clicking on that, in turn, takes you to a page that lists your area's support coordinators and contact information. Scroll down and you'll come to a list of support groups in your region, along with contact information for each, which may include the facilitator's phone number, an e-mail address and the meeting place and times. See if there is a local group you can contact. If there is none nearby, talk to the PSI state coordinator or consider starting your own group.

## HOW TO START A POSTPARTUM SUPPORT GROUP

Some women may live in areas that do not have postpartum support groups. Perhaps you have already talked to the PSI coordinator in your state and there is simply no group nearby. If you appear to live in a place where there are no postpartum organizations, check with your health professionals—obstetrician-gynecologist, pediatrician, midwife, doula, lactation consultant and local hospital—to find someone who might know of a local support group for mothers with postpartum depression. If you still can't find one, it may be up to you to start a group yourself! This may sound overwhelming, but there are resources for you to turn to. Just because there's no group in your area, that doesn't mean no one else is suffering from postpartum depression. The very process of putting together a group can be a great way to further your own recovery.

Begin by contacting Postpartum Support International and indicating that you're interested in starting a support group in your area. You can also contact the PSI coordinator in the state where you live for help in setting up a group. The *PSI Guidebook on Developing a Sustainable Perinatal Support Network in Your Community*, available for purchase on the PSI Web site, is a joint effort by PSI founder Jane Honikman and ten social service organizations in the United States and Canada. The booklet, covering how to start a support group, is written in a simple outline format and includes an appendix with samples of useful materials to get you started.

Another valuable booklet is *A Guide to Starting and Maintaining a Depression After Delivery (DAD) Support Group*, developed by Depression After Delivery, Inc., in cooperation with the New Jersey and American Self-Help Clearinghouse. It gives step-by-step instructions and suggestions for many essential tasks: locating a meeting place, recruiting group members, designing a group format and guidelines for discussions, holding your first meeting, handling difficult behavior at meetings, dealing with a crisis within your group, keeping the group active and providing online support.

Some books on postpartum depression also address the topic of support groups. *Postpartum Depression Demystified: An Essential Guide for Understanding and Overcoming the Most Common Complication after Childbirth* by Joyce Venis, a certified registered nurse, and Suzanne McCloskey, as well as *Postpartum Depression for Dummies* by Shoshana Bennett, PhD, include information.

Another tactic is to find an existing support group, even if you have to travel a bit to get there and connect with the leader. She may be willing to guide you, give you tips to get your own group started and allow you to sit in and observe some of her meetings. Over the years of leading my support group, numerous women interested in launching their own groups have contacted me for assistance. In these situations, after getting permission from the participants in my group, I extend an invitation for the women to attend a few meetings and learn about running a group. I also provide the women with copies of my support group guidelines and publicity flyer.

## Postpartum Anxiety/Depression Support Group Guidelines

*Facilitator:*
Susan Benjamin Feingold, PsyD

### *About the Group:*

- A free postpartum anxiety/depression support group will meet for six weeks on Wednesday afternoons from 1:00 to 2:30 at Family Network in Highland Park.
- One of the primary purposes of the support group is to provide an environment whereby women with postpartum depression or postpartum anxiety can meet with one another and help each other to cope during this stressful time in a supportive, caring and non-judgmental atmosphere.

### *Member Guidelines:*

1. Help other group members to feel comfortable and accepted.
2. Listen attentively and without interrupting when another member is speaking.
3. Participate in discussing and sharing problems as well as offering ideas (when appropriate).
4. It's not always necessary to offer advice; sometimes we just want someone to listen and be empathic.
5. Allow members to vent their sad and angry feelings without being judgmental.
6. Recognize that in a support group, the success of a group is not the sole responsibility of the group leader, but is the responsibility of the whole group.
7. Maintaining confidentiality is crucial for members to feel safe and be open to sharing.

**Postpartum Anxiety/Depression**
**Support Group Flyer**

- Insomnia
- Worrying
- Mood swings
- Extreme fatigue
- Severe anxiety
- Appetite loss
- Low self-esteem
- Obsessive thoughts

If you have any of the above symptoms, you could be experiencing Postpartum Depression or Anxiety. PPD affects 10–20% of all new mothers. It can occur anytime within the first year after delivery.

This group provides an environment where women with postpartum depression or anxiety can meet one another and help each other in a supportive, caring and non-judgmental atmosphere.

Susan Benjamin Feingold, PsyD, leads this 6-week support group at the Family Network Parent/Child Center.

Wednesdays 1:00-2:30 p.m.

Call for Registration and Information
847-831-7731

Family Network, a Family Focus Center, is a not-for-profit, non-sectarian, family support agency open to all.

Family Network
330 Laurel Avenue
Highland Park, IL 60035
847-433-0377

## Alice's Story

*I scheduled my first appointment with Alice, a woman who had grown up in a Mennonite area of Ohio and in a deeply religious family. Her case reminds me that postpartum depression is a nondiscriminatory illness.*

*Within two days of Alice's call, I was sitting in my office waiting for her to arrive. I had pictured her as small-framed, wearing a long, old-fashioned gingham skirt and white lace bonnet. I could not have been more wrong. Alice was a young woman of medium height, slim, extraordinarily pretty and dressed stylishly in black slacks and a wraparound sweater. She told me that her family was actually quite modern; no one wore bonnets or long dresses except those in her community who, like her maternal grandmother, were part of the Old Order Mennonites. She explained that most people of her faith didn't dress any differently from the general population.*

*Alice had moved away from her family to attend college, where she ended up meeting her husband, Robert, who was also a Mennonite and college educated. Later, as his professional career advanced, she traveled with him to Illinois.*

*Although Alice appeared to be very young, she was thirty-one years old and had five children, the youngest—and only girl—just three months old. Like many of my clients, she had been referred to me by both her obstetrician-gynecologist and the local hospital's perinatal hotline in response to her symptoms and the desperation in her voice.*

*She described a long history of difficult and complicated pregnancies and several miscarriages in between. With her most recent child, she started to hemorrhage at the beginning of the second trimester, necessitating months of bed rest. During that time, she feared she would lose the baby and intrusive memories of her prior miscarriages dominated her thoughts.*

*Alice indicated that she had always had a fair amount of anxiety. But when faced with the possibility of losing her baby girl and perhaps even her own life, that apprehension multiplied. She was aware that her husband was feeling a lot of pressure, too; as she lay in bed, unable to care for their other children or do the housework, and with the rest of her family so far away, Robert was left to tend to the children and the house, on top of the long hours he already spent working and commuting. Alice never shared with him or anyone else the degree of fear she experienced and the scary images she envisioned as she lay in bed during much of her pregnancy. She felt that to be a good wife she needed to sacrifice her emotions and not burden her husband. So she kept her worries to herself. This drive to be a good wife had been instilled in Alice since childhood, when her mother preached that it was extremely important for a good marital relationship and a healthy family life.*

*It turned out that Robert was struggling as well and, like Alice, never shared his feelings. He was trying his best to support her emotionally but was frightened that if he stayed home, he might lose his job and then wouldn't be able to support the family financially. Alice and Robert had always been close and were committed to their marriage, their family and each other. Yet, by both of them trying to protect the other, they never communicated their level of anxiety and kept most of their thoughts and feelings to themselves. This made them feel disconnected and alone at a time when they could have leaned on each other for emotional support.*

*It is not helpful for people to bottle up their feelings, even if it's for noble reasons or to save someone else from a burden. People can hold back only so long before their true sentiments start to surface as resentment, eruptions of anger or symptoms of anxiety. Eventually one's feelings seem to explode at the other person and the two get into an argument or one's feelings manifest in physical symptoms of stress, such as stomach aches, irritable bowel syndrome, heart palpitations and difficulty in breathing. Even with good intentions, holding back so as not to strain the other person often results in negative interactions or stress-induced conditions.*

*"I held it together as best I could," Alice recalled, "but inside I felt like a failure as a wife and a mother." She explained to me, "I couldn't help wondering what I was doing having another child when I wasn't even able to care for those that I already had."*

*Because of their strong marriage and commitment to their family, Alice and Robert worked to overcome the trials and experiences of Alice's pregnancy. They were reluctant to ask for favors, but since their circumstances were desperate, because of their four young children and an abundance of needs, they contacted their church friends and pastor for help. Even though they had lived in the area for less than a year (another stressor), the church was willing to provide support, in part by sending hot meals and helping with child care.*

*Alice had close ties to her family, but because they lived so far away and their own finances were limited, they were unable to visit and help out for more than a week. Alice felt deserted by her family, friends, spouse and religious community back home. This, too, led to alienation and loneliness during a critical period. Despite her faith, she could not help being angry and resentful—and then feeling guilty about having those feelings.*

*The importance of a support network becomes apparent when people face stressful challenges; postpartum illness is one of those ordeals. The lack of a support system is one of several factors that put women at risk for depression. Having friends, family and even caring community relationships within your church, synagogue or mosque can go a long way toward helping you cope if you are already suffering from postpartum depression or anxiety.*

*As I listened to her story, I could not help thinking that Alice had placed herself in a double bind. Her belief system did not allow her to feel angry or resentful at her spouse, family or friends. However, she could not dismiss these emotions. As hard as she tried to deny them, she found herself feeling resentful and was left with a complicated mix of guilt, shame and self-loathing. In the field of psychology, this is often known as cognitive dissonance, which occurs when there is a conflict between one's inner beliefs and outward behavior.*

*Additionally, Alice said that her faith was wavering, which added to her confusion and the complexity of her emotions. The Mennonite church values service and sacrifice, which are regarded as important means of expressing one's faith. Understanding this helped me recognize what a complicated predicament Alice was in.*

*She was also contending with mixed feelings over her mother's role model as a self-sacrificing woman, which reinforced Alice's faith-driven values. While her mother's actions may have been motivated by Mennonite religious principles, from Alice's comments they also seem to have been due to her mother's lack of self-worth. Alice revealed to me that her mother acted like a martyr, always letting Alice and her siblings know how much she sacrificed for them. She seemed to take pride in telling the children how she put their needs and those of their father above her own. This always annoyed Alice and made her feel bad, she told me, because she saw how her mother failed to take care of her appearance and health. Even though Alice told herself that she didn't want to live this way—that it was not healthy—she found herself feeling guilty whenever she took time for herself.*

*As a therapist, I have to consider a client's symptoms within the context of her religious and cultural background, rather than as unique attributes or just an individual's pathology. In addition to considering cross-cultural mores, it's important to take into account a person's family of origin and the influence of family patterns and relationships while growing up. In the case of Alice, when we understand her religious upbringing and belief system, we gain a very different perspective on her need to sacrifice and to serve her spouse and children.*

*Despite all the confusing messages from her past as well as her present concerns, Alice never asked for professional help and no one knew what she was thinking or what conflicts she was struggling with. Consequently, no one reached out to help her. From her description of that time, however, I think it's likely that Alice was suffering from antepartum depression and anxiety. Had she sought help then, instead of waiting until three months postpartum, she could have received early intervention.*

*Why does that matter? Because the earlier a woman gets assessment and treatment, generally speaking, the better her prognosis and the shorter her recovery time. This is not to say that women who come for treatment later do not get well. But the situation becomes more complicated the longer someone is ill and that often translates into a lengthier course of treatment and more time spent suffering.*

*As hard as Alice's pregnancy had been, however, things did not improve with delivery. Labor was long and difficult and after twenty-three hours the doctor determined that the fetus was in distress and Alice was quickly prepared for a Cesarean section. This seemed to confirm her feelings of failure and belief that she couldn't do anything right. She decided she had failed as a mom and now she couldn't even deliver the baby naturally.*

*After a short hospital stay, Alice returned home to face caring for four young children in addition to her newborn. Robert was given a new project at work that required longer hours at the office and extra time traveling out of town, so he was largely unavailable. He felt bad about the situation, but as sole breadwinner for a family of seven, he didn't think he could risk losing his job. Alice again felt abandoned. Still, she was reluctant to speak up about her emotions. She was even feeling resentful toward the baby and noticed that she was not attaching or bonding with her daughter as she had with her other children.*

*As her isolation and anxiety about being alone with the children grew, her symptoms of depression and anxiety did, too. In addition, she felt that she had never had a real chance to rest and heal after the Cesarean section and now she was experiencing physical problems, like pain in her legs and at the incision site. Breast-feeding was not going well either, likely due to her exhaustion. It is not difficult to imagine how all of this added to her feelings of failure and hopelessness.*

*After a few weeks, her mother and sister came to see the new baby and help out for two weeks. Alice began to feel better with the extra support and their encouragement that she was doing a good job. Still, they noticed that she was not her usual cheerful self and expressed their concern to her husband. Robert was worried, but he didn't know what to do: Was it was better to talk to his wife about her feelings or just ignore it? He chose not to discuss it directly, as he feared that Alice might get more upset if she knew everyone noticed her foul mood. Instead, he lent a hand with the children when he could and encouraged his wife to call her family and see church friends more often. This helped a little but not enough to turn around her growing clinical depression. And with her mother and sister gone, Alice began to feel desperate and lonely again.*

*As the weeks wore on, her symptoms worsened. Alice kept thinking that if she could just be a good wife and mother, sacrifice for her children and pray, she would get better. But she felt more and more detached from her children and disconnected from her husband. She stopped going to church, seeing friends and calling family in Ohio, because she didn't want to admit that she was getting worse but neither did she have the energy to fake it.*

*At around three months postpartum, Alice had one particularly stressful morning when she could not get her daughter down for a nap. As she gazed at the infant, she suddenly had the terrifying thought that she might hurt the baby; in fact, she decided that she should not be entrusted with any of the children. This was followed by panic and intrusive, frightening thoughts that everyone would be better off without her, so she should take her own life. That's when Alice finally knew she needed professional help. She called her ob-gyn and was referred to me and the local hospital's perinatal hotline.*

*During my first appointment with Alice, I gathered information about her and explained the symptoms of postpartum depression and anxiety. Sometimes just providing information about postpartum illness goes a long way toward helping a client feel less frightened, "crazy" and hopeless. This was certainly true in Alice's case.*

*Following our initial meeting, we established a regular weekly schedule of sessions and began working on decreasing her symptoms of depression and anxiety. We discussed interventions that can be helpful with obsessive thoughts and we practiced relaxation and breathing techniques to help her allay her anxiety and panic. I also provided a safe, nonjudgmental environment where she could explore some of her conflicting feelings about parenting, her belief system and her family relationships. I referred her to a psychiatrist who was experienced in treating perinatal depression and, with a little encouragement, Alice agreed to give medication a try.*

*Within a few sessions, we both could see progress in Alice and her symptoms began decreasing in intensity. However, the first signs of recovery can represent a dangerous time, when many women are prone to terminate treatment prematurely. Although I often encourage women to taper the frequency of their treatments at this point, just to see whether they can maintain their improvement with a little less support, they need to understand that some recovery is not enough; they should continue regular psychotherapy, even if it's less often.*

*Alice's biggest challenge still lay ahead. She had such a strong model of self-deprivation, perfectionism and self-sacrifice that we needed to address these issues directly. I knew that if she continued to feel guilty for nurturing herself or for taking time to be alone, all her recent hard work to heal would probably be just a temporary fix and she would exhaust herself right back into poor health and, likely, depression. Her difficulty taking time for herself and countering some of the parental modeling, faith-based values and messages learned in childhood made this task particularly hard. I wanted to be sensitive to her religious beliefs. Even though, on a cognitive level, Alice could see her weary mother as a victim of her own martyrdom, in reality Alice still bought into much of the same thinking and behavior. Her guilt when she thought she had been self-indulgent was the cornerstone holding this belief system in place.*

*Another issue to address was Alice's feeling of alienation and her social withdrawal from her family, her friends and, most crucially, her husband.*

*I regularly encourage my clients, within their first few appointments, to bring their spouses or significant others to one of our sessions. I've found this to be so valuable in educating a client's partner, in observing how they relate as a couple and in gathering information from someone who observes the client regularly and who knew the spouse intimately before the illness, that it has become a standard part of the therapy I practice. It lets me evaluate how the partner is holding up and sometimes, when needed, leads to a referral for the spouse to seek individual treatment or the couple to consider marital therapy.*

*After a few appointments, I suggested that she bring Robert with her. Although he was working long hours, he made arrangements to attend, because he was committed to his wife and their relationship. Additionally, he had noticed an improvement since Alice had begun treatment. During the session, their interactions were loving and they focused initially on general questions about postpartum depression. However, once their comfort level rose, Robert finally opened up about how difficult the pregnancy, new baby and Alice's postpartum depression had been for him, too. That seemed to unlock the floodgates: Soon both of them were crying, admitting that they had each been struggling but were holding in their feelings to protect the other one. Finally came confessions of resentment and anger.*

*By encouraging Alice and Robert to break through the isolation each was feeling and to communicate directly and honestly, the session improved their connectedness significantly. They could work together as a couple again. It also allowed Robert to understand what was ailing Alice, which reduced his anxiety and helped her to feel heard.*

*As Alice's symptoms subsided over the following months, she was able to address the factors that had made her vulnerable to depression in the first place. That, in turn, allowed her to identify the positive outcome and search for meaning in her postpartum experience. She realized that her mother's self-sacrifice and poor self-care had eroded her self-esteem but also had been an attempt to bolster it by enabling her to "guilt" Alice and the other children into assisting her in various ways.*

*As soon as Alice had this epiphany, she started to change so she would not repeat the pattern with her own children. She began to take better care of herself and was able to do this for the first time without feeling guilty. She realized that her mother was not perfect but accepted her as "a woman just doing the best she could." This allowed her to confront her own perfectionism and work on being authentically Alice and a "good enough" mom. She and Robert continued to communicate more openly and directly with each other, leading ultimately to a better marriage.*

*We continued treatment on a weekly basis and Alice made greater and greater strides in her mental health. Although my tendency is to gradually reduce the frequency of sessions once I begin to see improvement, she and I agreed to use this opportunity to explore in depth some of her family issues, which had contributed to her current difficulties. She felt a loyalty to her family members and did not want to bad-mouth them, she said. It was a challenge for her to discuss kin-related matters with an "outsider," as she put it, without tremendous guilt. After all, I was not a Mennonite and she had been raised to be silent with others about private family matters. Fiercely loyal, Alice was likely afraid that I might think badly of her mother, family or religious community. She knew that I'd had limited exposure to people of the Mennonite faith and she didn't want to paint an unpleasant picture or engender negative bias.*

*But as her symptoms abated and she became healthier, Alice trusted me more and opened up in treatment. Our therapeutic alliance deepened and, putting aside her concerns over what I would think of her relatives, she confided more about her early relationship with her mother. She admitted that even when she was a child, her mom used to talk to her the way one speaks to a therapist, divulging intimate facts about her marriage and personal problems and revealing other information—financial woes, problems in her friendships, insecurities—beyond what should be discussed with a young daughter. Even as she listened, young Alice knew that it was inappropriate to be her mother's sounding board; her mom should not have been exposing her to all these personal adult matters. Yet what was Alice to do? Her reaction was to foster a great resentment over being her mother's confidante and being burdened with this private world of "secrets." As in other family matters, Alice was ambivalent about her "special" role. On one hand, it was an honor to be chosen to hear these grown-up things and it made her feel important; on the other hand, it made her uncomfortable to be given details that no child her age had any business knowing or worrying about.*

*Reflecting back on those years, Alice experienced both anger at her mother's lack of boundaries and sadness that her mom never received the professional help she could have used. Seeing a therapist would have also served as a good example to Alice and saved her the undue responsibility of being a "parental child" (a youngster who assumes a parental role in a family).*

*"It was too much responsibility for a kid to have and it only became more intense over the years," Alice recalled. Sometimes it got so bad that Alice avoided being alone with her mom; she even went to school when she was ill rather than spend hours at home listening to her mom complain, which made Alice feel worse. When she got older and moved away, her mother often called her on the phone and talked for hours about her troubles, leaving Alice drained but too guilty to tell her mom she didn't want to hear about her problems anymore.*

*Alice's postpartum depression seemed to coincide with an increase in these phone calls. She was unsure how great a factor they played in her illness, but it didn't help her own anxiety or depression to hear about her mother's difficulties. Eventually Alice decided she had to stop being used to satisfy her mother's neediness. "I just can't be her therapist any longer," she explained to me. "Now I have my own family and five young children to take care of."*

*As we explored these issues over the next few months, Alice began to realize that although the blueprint for her relationship with her mother had been set in childhood, her own codependence and tendency toward excessive caretaking were the reasons she continued enabling her mom's inappropriate behavior. (According to the APA Dictionary of Psychology, codependence is a dysfunctional relationship pattern in which two individuals are emotionally dependent on one another.)*

*Alice acknowledged her own responsibility in maintaining this unhealthy relationship. She realized that if things were going to change, she would have to take the lead. And so she did. She set boundaries, encouraged her mother to talk to a professional therapist and let her mom know that she resented having been put in the position of "intimate friend" when she was only a child. Alice also made it clear that she would no longer play the role of confidante.*

---

Through her hard work, Alice developed a healthy adult relationship with her mother and forgave the past hurt. This led to a transformation: She was no longer enabling her mother's constant sacrifice. Nor was Alice sacrificing herself or filled with guilt when she set boundaries or felt angry. She let go of her past and became a happier, healthier woman.

*PART III*

# PRINCIPLES FOR HEALING, GROWING AND FINDING MEANING FROM POSTPARTUM DEPRESSION

# CHAPTER 7

## *Finding Meaning*

A question my clients often ask early on is, "Why is this happening to me?" Implicit is the hope that I can help them acquire some significant meaning from their experiences, some purpose for their suffering. An additional question embedded in the *why* is, "Will I ever be healthy again?" During the beginning phase of treatment, this query is premature. We cannot know yet what change or personal growth will result.

You most likely have similar questions. In order to answer the why question, you will need to be further along in the healing process or even healed. However, in time you will know the answers to a series of questions: How has this experience changed you? How have you grown? What have you learned?

In the next chapters, I focus on the principles that are necessary in order to get well, grow and find personal meaning or significance through postpartum depression. I include stories from women who have recovered from the condition and are now able to answer those questions for themselves.

It seems to be hardwired in us to search for meaning in our experiences and, ultimately, in our lives. Philosophers, scientists and theologians have struggled with these issues throughout time. Numerous books on spirituality and psychology have addressed these concerns. Suffering often makes us more introspective and shifts our focus from the material aspects of life to more profound ones: Since the physical goods we own can't bring us joy, superficial possessions lose their allure; they may even feel distasteful or burdensome and we're no longer drawn to them. We search for answers elsewhere instead—in other people and our own selves.

The human need to find meaning typically emerges during certain life stages, like adolescence/young adulthood, when we are creating our identities. This is played out most noticeably in the need to choose a livelihood. Young people often look for a career that will be meaningful and satisfying and can meet not only their personal goals but their altruistic ambitions as well. Others find purpose outside of their work, perhaps in volunteer activities or social causes. The process can be grueling and painful. It can trigger an existential crisis in some, as they grapple to give their lives significance.

The hunt for meaning becomes apparent during other times, too, such as choosing a life partner, marriage and parenthood. Other points of searching for meaning can come in middle age, which can give rise to a midlife crisis, and in elder adulthood, when we contemplate our very existence and the definitive value of our life as we move into our final years. As Marianne Williamson writes in *The Age of Miracles,* "No matter who we are, we have things we're supposed to do to fulfill the calling of our souls. But the soul's calling isn't a broad revelation that will be written in large letters across the sky. Rather, it's a challenge to be the person we're capable of being in any given moment."[1]

Your struggle with postpartum depression represents just such a pivotal time in your own life. Whatever your calling, whether to help others or change the world, you now have an opportunity to give meaning to your experience and create something positive from it.

For all of us, there are certainly times that are tremendously painful. Yet it is often out of these difficulties that we find our personal strength and the capacity for change and growth. I believe that we change more when we make mistakes and undergo pain than when things are smooth and easy. As has often been said, we are a product of our mistakes. The present "you" is an accumulation of all you have experienced, including all your blunders and hard times. How can your postpartum depression not have a dramatic effect on you? It would be hard to undergo something so intense without changing remarkably. Many positive events have an impact on your life, too. But when you think about who you are now, it's often the intense, more painful memories that come to mind and seem to affect you to your core.

During a new client's first appointment, I always ask, "What are some of your significant life events?" Rarely does someone report a fun vacation, a great talk with a friend or a special birthday party. Instead, she talks about the loss of her first love, divorce, childhood abuse, grief over the death of a loved one, a traumatic delivery. These rough times are what stand out in people's minds. It's these difficult, negative experiences that have a significant impact and change us. Even in the case of a client who cited winning the lottery as a significant life event, what altered her life was not the fact that she now had enough money to buy a new house, pay for her children's educations, take a vacation or adopt a better lifestyle, but rather the effect the money had on her relationships. Besides hearing from long-lost relatives who wanted to share in her wealth, friends became envious of her, she said, and thought she had moved into a different social class.

Sometimes the transformation that follows postpartum depression can be life altering, but other times the shift is mainly a change in attitude. Leslie's story reveals this shift.

---

### Leslie's Story

*Leslie, a thirty-two-year-old woman, had a three-week-old baby boy, her first child and the result of a planned and much-desired pregnancy. Although she was married for only a year, she had lived with her future husband for the previous five years and they had known each other since elementary school. She described her husband as supportive and her best friend and reported that they had a good marriage.*

*Leslie had lived in Chicago for seven years, having moved there after college. She and her husband had grown up in a small Midwestern town where both of their families continued to live. Although she was from a close-knit family, she said she was independent and self-reliant. When she first arrived in Chicago, she was single and on her own, with no friends. Over the past few years, she had built up a good network of friends and became well liked at her job as a supervisor in a large corporation. Leslie was successful at work, had an active, satisfying social life and a good marriage. She appeared to be self-confident despite her postpartum symptoms.*

*Leslie had never before been in psychotherapy and stated that she hadn't experienced any prior depression. She reported that she was generally not very anxious and previously had not suffered from anxiety. As discussed previously, depression can often first appear as anxiety. Furthermore, postpartum depression frequently presents as an anxious depression.*

*Two weeks after her delivery, Leslie stopped nursing because the baby had difficulty latching on. Subsequently, she began to experience episodes of crying, feelings of anxiety, low and depressed moods, guilt, loss of appetite, a significant amount of worrying, ruminating and fears about being alone with the baby as well as a loss of interest and pleasure. Leslie tried to use all her good coping skills, but when nothing helped, she became alarmed and quickly took action by calling her physician, who referred her to me for an evaluation and possible treatment.*

*Leslie described her family to me as being cohesive and intact and having good work values. She stated that her parents had a good marriage but described them as a little old-fashioned with traditional gender roles. Her father was the breadwinner and it was largely her mother who had been responsible for taking care of the children and running the household. Leslie's older and younger sisters still lived in the same town where they grew up. She indicated that her childhood was happy and she continued to feel that her family was loving and supportive.*

*As we talked, she reported that she always felt physically strong, emotionally stable and had never experienced extreme mood symptoms before, with the exception of, in her words, "a little moodiness" around her menstrual cycle. Leslie said she felt lucky to live a comfortable, middle-class life. She felt fortunate that she had close, loving relationships with family and friends, a good job and a stable marriage and was even blessed with a "good, even-tempered" baby, as she put it. Her pregnancy was planned, no fertility treatment was necessary, and she had felt emotionally healthy throughout her pregnancy.*

*As can be expected with a well-adjusted, emotionally stable and healthy person, she never had psychotherapy before and never thought that she would be the type of person to seek help, particularly from a therapist. She and those who knew her were surprised when a few weeks after her delivery she became seriously depressed. It was only because of her own desperation and failed attempts to help herself that she finally agreed to talk to a therapist and called me (with a referral from her physician and the insistence of her spouse and relatives).*

*According to Leslie, things generally went her way, which she felt was partly because she planned her future and partly just because she was fortunate and not prone to mishaps. She truly believed that "bad things just don't happen to me."*

*After relating these facts at our first appointment, she asked me, "So what happened? How did this happen to me?"*

*It's interesting and yet strange how we think we're invincible. This erroneous belief keeps us feeling safe and unaware of our vulnerability. We prefer to assume, as Leslie did, that something like postpartum depression could never happen to us. We read dramatic and sensational stories of women with severe cases of postpartum depression who sometimes, out of despair, take desperate measures and yet we tell ourselves, This could never happen to me.*

*I wish I could say that's true, that you are safe or somehow different. Unfortunately, that's not what I have found. While there are people who are at greater risk for a depressive episode because they have a genetic vulnerability (one of several risk factors I've discussed), multiple factors contribute to a postpartum emotional disorder and many clients who develop the condition have no history of depression or anxiety and have never visited a therapist before.*

*Leslie responded very well to a short course of psychotherapy, as could be expected with her mental health history (no prior incidents of depression or severe anxiety) and minimal stressors. The risk factors that I identified, which may have been responsible for her postpartum episode, were the lack of emotional support (her close-knit family was out of state and thus not readily available to help her), high sensitivity to changes in hormone levels (as evidenced by her moodiness or PMS during menstrual cycles) and the fact that her abrupt cessation of breast-feeding seemed to precipitate her postpartum depression.*

*Following her episode, which was intense but relatively short, Leslie confided that she had learned some significant things and felt that she had changed as a result of what she went through. She proceeded to tell me about her previous tendency to be quite critical of others, particularly those with mental health problems like depression, anxiety or panic attacks. She assumed that the person was "weak in character, screwed up or somehow different from me."*

*This was particularly interesting in light of the fact that my client was generally very positive and optimistic.*

*I suspected that most of her friends and colleagues*

*were never aware of this critical side and would have been surprised to hear of it. Leslie described an "awakening" when she began to admit to herself and me a lack of empathy for people whose mental health was less fortunate. This seemed to be the one area where she was judgmental of others.*

*It was only out of Leslie's own episode of depression that she began to know how clinical depression felt. Her postpartum depression awakened her empathic side as she realized that depression isn't something one can push away with a good attitude or by trying harder. It also taught her that she's not invincible and although she's been healthy so far, she shouldn't take either her mental or her physical health for granted.*

*Was this experience life-altering for Leslie? Yes. She matured and became more empathic and tolerant of others. You may even say that she underwent a type of metamorphosis. Did others see her as different? Probably not. However, she knew that the experience had changed her in a personally profound way and she was able to admit that to herself and to me.*

---

For certain clients, the change is obvious or at least observable, while for others it's more subtle and less noticeable, such as a shift in attitude. As I indicated earlier, if treatment is brief, the therapist may get only a snapshot of the mother during a particularly difficult period. Sometimes, women I treat in short-term therapy go through an experience such as postpartum depression and I never learn how it affects them. However, I believe that, even when the episode is short, it alters them in some way. Even though I don't always know the long-term effects, I feel strongly that postpartum depression is never the end of the story: An experience as intense as this must alter life significantly. Many times when I treat a woman for a longer period, perhaps a few months, I am better able to see the result of this experience. In those cases, I have the privilege of hearing about the metamorphosis from the client's own mouth.

## KAREN'S STORY

*Karen was referred to me by her obstetrician-gynecologist, who was concerned about Karen's level of anxiety and frequent calls, which seemed excessive for a first-time mother only eleven weeks postpartum. She also presented with signs of depressive disorder. Karen was lucky to have an informed physician who became concerned about her behavior. Sometimes healthcare providers miss the signs of postpartum depression when women with postpartum anxiety disorder don't show "typical" depressive symptoms, such as crying and sadness. It is not uncommon for these clients never to be properly diagnosed or referred for treatment.*

*At her intake appointment, Karen said that when she was about eight weeks postpartum, she began to worry and feel intense anxiety. Her sleep, when she got any, was poor: very light and punctuated by nights of initial insomnia or early morning awakening (that is, waking in the early hours and being unable to fall back to sleep). Previously, she had been a high-functioning, respected radiologist at a reputable medical center. But now even mundane household and childcare tasks were hard for her. Karen was scheduled to return to work part-time in just a week and full-time shortly thereafter, so it was understandable that her anxiety was increasing. She was especially concerned that the complexity of her job exceeded her current ability. She was overwhelmed about the upcoming pressure of her work, the ongoing demands of her infant daughter and the disconnection she felt from her former self.*

*Karen reported having difficulty paying attention to tasks, making simple decisions, remembering things short term and even concentrating enough to follow TV sitcoms and simple articles in popular magazines. She had even begun bursting uncontrollably into tears, though it seemed unrelated to her present life. She didn't know how she could function like this at work and she worried that her colleagues would think she was unstable. Worse, she feared she might damage her professional reputation, lose her job or inadvertently harm a patient. Karen also suffered from painful memories of her child's birth, which she described as "very stressful," and had frightening thoughts that "something was wrong" with her infant daughter, as she put it. This exacerbated her worry and made her panicky.*

*During an intake session, I often use the Edinburgh Postnatal Depression Scale to screen a client prior to treatment. This gives the client an objective measure to substantiate my diagnosis. I retest again at the conclusion of therapy and compare the two scores. Clients get to see their progress objectively. Karen scored nineteen on the Edinburgh scale, which is clinically significant for postpartum depression and similar to the results I've seen for other clients with moderate to moderately severe postpartum depression.*

*A few days following our initial session, Karen canceled her second appointment, saying she disagreed with my diagnosis and felt better; she had decided she didn't need therapy after all. She was trying to convince herself that all she was dealing with was sleep deprivation, adjusting to being married "only a year" and having a new baby.*

*I may never have heard from Karen again had it not been for a bad case of flu she contracted. While laid up for days, she ruminated about the baby's health and started to experience a great deal of panic and anxiety. When Karen finally recovered from the flu, she was so upset that she decided to schedule another appointment with me and reconsider her previous decision.*

*She seemed visibly shaken in our second session. She began a course of psychotherapy and, ultimately, a long-term therapeutic relationship that waxed and waned over the next decade, during which I treated*

*Karen for two postpartum depressions, post-traumatic stress disorder from an abusive childhood and relationship issues with her spouse.*

*It is common for clients to stay in therapy only long enough for their depression to go into remission. (This is commonly referred to as short-term therapy.) While certainly appropriate, if a client continues with "deeper work," she can make tremendous advances in personal growth. Karen is a good example of this latter type of client.*

*During our first two appointments Karen related that her pregnancy had been uneventful; she had felt healthy, strong, even "blissful" at times. It was a planned first pregnancy and she had no prior pregnancies, miscarriages or abortions. Karen described the delivery as painful and said that she yelled and screamed a lot. She felt embarrassed and somewhat humiliated that she had behaved in such an undignified fashion in front of the medical team and her husband.*

*During and immediately after the birth, some unforeseen and particularly stressful events occurred. The nursing staff and Karen's physician thought they noticed a cardiac arrhythmia in the baby. Later, when Karen's husband, John, was in the nursery to peek in on his daughter sleeping peacefully, a doctor walked in and abruptly demanded of a nurse nearby, "Where's the newborn with the heart problem?" He was directed to Karen and John's child. The nurse was obviously uncomfortable with the physician's insensitivity and quietly pointed out the father. Now somewhat sheepish, the doctor introduced himself to John as a pediatrician who had been called in to examine the child. The well-meaning nurses wanted an infant specialist to examine the baby before they approached the parents with what would surely be distressing news.*

*John was noticeably disturbed when he related this to his wife later. Karen was equally traumatized. The baby was kept in the hospital for observation and testing while the parents returned home in a state of shock and horror. It was several days before the baby was released and the diagnosis of cardiac arrhythmia dismissed. But to Karen it seemed like weeks and she couldn't ignore the possibility that something was indeed wrong with her child's health.*

*Karen revealed to me, "I feel like I was cheated out of a happy childbirth experience." Despite the positive health report, over the next few months she continued to worry about the baby and felt extreme apprehension over a potential problem that wasn't readily visible. She obsessed that the doctors had been wrong and found herself checking the baby's chest frequently throughout the day and night for signs of an irregular heartbeat. This concern led to Karen's significant anxiety and frequent calls to her pediatrician's office.*

*My diagnosis for Karen was more than just postpartum depression; it included anxiety, obsessive-compulsive disorder (OCD) and post-traumatic stress disorder (PTSD). Anxiety, as well as panic, OCD and PTSD, which are various kinds of anxiety disorders, can occur alongside postpartum depression, either by themselves or in combination. When any of them show up together, postpartum depression is often called postpartum anxiety disorder, postpartum panic disorder or postpartum OCD, depending upon the predominant symptom or symptoms. Rather than looking at these anxiety disorders as distinct from postpartum depression, I see them as different subtypes of the depression, whether or not they occur simultaneously with it. There appears to be depression in most instances of postpartum anxiety, although it may be "under the surface" or overshadowed by the anxiety symptoms. Often when there seem to be symptoms only of anxiety, as I begin to treat the client, indications of depression surface, too. Perhaps the depression was just eclipsed by the anxiety and as that diminishes I can see the depression more clearly. Other times, the predominant symptoms are irritability and anger; these women usually view themselves as bad mothers instead of recognizing that they have an irritable type of clinical depression.*

*You may think Karen's anxiety started with the trauma of learning, shortly after childbirth, that her daughter might have a heart condition. That experience seems to have led to postpartum depression, along with obsessive thoughts that her child really did have a congenital heart defect. Was it post-traumatic stress disorder that set off her postpartum illness?*

*Whenever we find a traumatic incident around a birth, we assume that's what triggered the depression. But how can anyone know what would have happened in the absence of the stress? Would the woman have stayed healthy? It's all conjecture. As you read more of Karen's story, you will see that her PTSD was a result not only of the emotional pain she suffered just after childbirth but also of growing up in a home filled with domestic violence and child abuse. The dynamics of Karen's early years and nuclear family turned out to be particularly relevant, because she apparently replicated them with her husband and child.*

*In the next few sessions, Karen described a long history of depression and anxiety, which she traced back to her childhood and adolescence, when she was dealing with her physically and emotionally abusive as well as controlling father. She was the only girl in an intact family with five older brothers. The term intact means her parents were married, not divorced, but it does not preclude dysfunction: Karen portrayed a scene of domestic violence. Her father disciplined her and her brothers harshly and beat her mother and all the children.*

*She told me that her mother, who was "very smart," had gone to college for a few years and was likely brighter than Karen's father. Yet over the course of her marriage, she had been beaten down into a quiet and submissive woman. Karen always suspected that her father felt intellectually inferior to her mother and used verbal abuse, put-downs and intimidation to make himself feel superior and her mother feel inadequate. This, along with having six children, is probably what kept Karen's mother in the marriage. Karen also reported, sadly, that her father was not very successful financially. He was always coming up with inventions that didn't amount to anything, she said, which only added to his frustration and low self-esteem and most likely a depression of his own.*

*Karen, however, did well in school, was accepted to her state university on a scholarship and moved away from her rural home. In college, she dated and had a few serious boyfriends but eventually moved to the Midwest to take a position at a well-respected hospital. She was successful in her job but lonely, being so far from family and friends in a big city where she knew no one. Within a few months she met John, the "man of her dreams," and they married after less than a year of dating. Karen thought he was "husband material": kind and stable, the sort of person who would be a good provider. But John was threatened by her intellect and higher level of education, a pattern she would come to recognize only later as similar to her parents' relationship.*

*John became more and more controlling over the years. When he left his job to start his own business with a partner, the added stress and financial insecurity increased the tension between him and Karen. Like Karen's father, John had a short fuse and was prone to angry tirades, which led to violent behavior, such as punching walls, throwing objects, yelling and intimidating his wife. Many of the couple's friends and neighbors viewed him as good-natured and an "all-around nice guy." But when he and Karen disagreed, he threw violent fits that reminded her of her father and frightened her. Karen was quick to point out to me that she didn't really see John as abusive: He never hit her, as her father had, although she admitted that he had kicked in the door on more than one occasion. John also criticized Karen and put her down in other ways, much as her own father had. He pointed out how inadequate she was as a mother, so different from the wives of his business partners and friends, to whom he often compared Karen. Over time, this criticism eroded her self-esteem and confidence as a mom and an individual. She began to believe she was an inadequate mother and became extremely tough on herself in many ways.*

*In an unconscious attempt to work out critical early relationships between themselves and their parents, people often marry someone quite similar to their mothers or fathers. Clients who are ordinarily bright and insightful frequently miss the signs that their prospective life mates have many of the same negative traits as one of their parents (often the one they have the most difficulty with). It wasn't until years later that Karen recognized the many signs that showed John shared numerous characteristics with her father. For example, she recalled that on a road trip once, early in their relationship, she accidentally made a wrong turn. John got so angry he punched the dashboard with his fist, frightening Karen. At the time, she didn't interpret the incident as an indication of bad temper or trouble ahead; she quickly forgot it. But oddly enough, perhaps it was these very similarities with her dad that made Karen see John as husband material.*

*Karen confided further during our sessions that over the course of her five-year marriage, John had become less interested in her romantically, rarely initiating sex and often refusing her when she suggested it. He used a variety of excuses: He was turned off to her during pregnancy, he found it repulsive to have sex with her while she was still breast-feeding, she had gotten "too fat" after childbirth to be attractive. Her self-esteem suffered and she felt less and less appealing and more and more stuck in an unhappy marriage. Just as her mother had done, Karen blamed herself and thought that if she were prettier, thinner, a better mother and wife then everything would be fine with her and John. After all, she told me, "everyone liked him" and saw him as an "easygoing, friendly, good guy." It was likely her fault that things were not better between them. This self-blame had been ingrained in her as a child, when she used to think, If only I were a good little girl, my father wouldn't be so angry and wouldn't have to hit me and say mean things to me.*

*I find it incredible—but also sad—that a woman as intelligent and professionally accomplished as Karen would put up with this type of intimidation and emotional abuse in her personal life. I wish I could report that this pattern is unusual; however, it speaks to the influence of our early years. It makes no difference how intelligent we are or how successful we become. Our childhood experiences have profound effects on us and the choices we make as adults. Karen, just like many other women I have treated, insisted she did not see this abusive pattern with her husband when they first met or married, that this pattern emerged only later in their relationship. I cannot explain how this happens, but it seems more than coincidence that people find themselves in relationships that repeat the family dynamics they learned as children from their parents. Although it seems to be a subconscious attempt to work through and correct the troubled early relationship, instead the same cycle of abuse is usually perpetuated until the client simply leaves the present-day relationship after becoming more psychologically healthy.*

*After a brief course of psychotherapy and medication, Karen's postpartum symptoms began to remit and she went back to her professional career and life with her husband and baby. At this point we tapered off treatment, going weeks between sessions.*

*This is an effective way to assess a client's progress and help her build the confidence that she is becoming healthy. It's a sure sign of growth when a client can go for weeks without therapy and still maintain emotional stability. In addition, it helps minimize dependence on the therapist and the therapeutic relationship in order to function and cope.*

*Once clients' symptoms go into full remission and the postpartum illness is over, I often offer three alternatives. First, they can terminate treatment following a final appointment to review our work together and discuss how to maintain good mental health. I let them know that they can always call me if they have mental health problems again. Second, they can schedule appointments as needed and "leave the door open" without a formal termination appointment. Third, they can continue treatment on a maintenance schedule, assuming they keep feeling okay. Clients on maintenance generally come in for sessions every four to six weeks and this helps them stay accountable for upholding healthy lifestyles and working on improving their lives. It also allows them to explore problems they're finally ready to deal with, such as deep issues arising from their youth and early relationships.*

*As time passed, I saw Karen even less frequently. She was feeling good, she reported, and besides being an involved new mom, she was back at her job. Some clients terminate treatment at this point, but Karen remained in therapy and kept the door open to working on getting healthier and keeping herself psychologically strong.*

*Slowly, Karen began to acknowledge and concentrate more on her relationship problems and marital discontent. She also opened up more about her early life within a dysfunctional family, specifically the childhood abuse she suffered, which she was unprepared to confront during our initial treatment when the focus was on her postpartum symptoms and adjustment to motherhood.*

*In discussing her marriage, Karen sometimes described dreams about old college boyfriends and past relationships in which she felt good about herself—feminine, attractive, desirable—as opposed to how she currently felt. Like many other women at this stage of their lives, Karen thought that things might improve if she and John had another child or waited until their daughter got older and they could refocus on each other.*

*Therapy continued to taper off and we met only once every few weeks. Sometimes months passed between sessions. When we met, we concentrated on Karen taking better care of herself, building self-esteem, maintaining good mental health and working to improve her rapport with John. We also began to address Karen's family dynamics and how her early relationships had affected her past decisions and present life. Although the marriage never improved significantly, Karen made considerable progress: She became more trusting, a better communicator and much more willing to explore issues on a deep level. In addition, she seemed more capable of intimate personal relationships, which allowed her to form satisfying bonds with friends and her daughter. But as Karen and John considered having a second child, she grew apprehensive about another episode of postpartum depression and anxiety and requested more frequent therapy sessions. Karen was correct to be concerned, for she was at high risk for a reoccurrence.*

*It is not unusual for a woman who experiences a significant postpartum depression to worry about another episode. In some cases, the original experience is so traumatic that she develops post-traumatic stress disorder. Although the incidence of postpartum emotional disorders is 10 to 20 percent among all childbearing women, this rate can increase up to 50 percent for women with a history of the disorder who become pregnant again. I have found that despite this risk, women can make a dramatic difference by taking preventive measures, such as going to individual psychotherapy sessions, adopting coping strategies, building a strong support network, establishing a postpartum plan and/or getting medication when necessary. By using some care of this type, many of my high-risk clients end up with less-severe episodes or none at all. Without any preventive measures, it is generally found that in a successive pregnancy, a woman is at risk for another episode and it can get more severe with each subsequent pregnancy.*

*After a few months trying to conceive, Karen became pregnant again and the couple moved out of the city to a larger house in a nearby suburb. As is usually the case, however, conceiving another child did not remedy their troubled marriage. Karen tried to persuade her husband to go to couple's therapy with her. But John said he didn't "believe" in it and felt like there was nothing wrong with him; it was Karen who needed to be "fixed."*

*Karen's second pregnancy was fraught with concerns about how she would manage her career, financial pressures and marriage along with two children. She was anxious about her ability to split her attention between her two-year-old and an infant, particularly since her daughter had recently become clingy, was prone to tantrums (which is common at this age) and was having difficulty separating from Karen. With the advice of her physician, she began taking a low-dose antidepressant, which seemed to help with her mood fluctuations, anxiety and obsessive thoughts.*

*Karen's mood improved gradually in the next few weeks. I observed her during periodic sessions and she was quite stable emotionally through the rest of her pregnancy. Following the delivery, Karen had minimal symptoms. I assessed her at two weeks postpartum and found her to be doing quite well. Therefore, we decided that she would monitor her own mood and if symptoms began she would call me to set up regular appointments. Because Karen was observant and psychologically minded (meaning savvy and well-versed in utilizing psychotherapy), I was confident that she would call me if she began to feel postpartum symptoms occurring. From two weeks postpartum until about five months after her second childbirth, we stopped treatment altogether. When Karen contacted me later that year to schedule appointments, it was to discuss the stress of raising two children, her growing dissatisfaction in her marriage and pressure from her job.*

*Karen had periodic symptoms of depressed and anxious moods for the next few years. This was often related to her troubled marriage. Although she admitted being dissatisfied in her relationship, she was not ready to give up on it. She continued seeing me every few weeks and worked on strengthening herself and her professional career as well as on being a good mother, despite her husband's ongoing negative messages. She sometimes minimized the impact her relationship was having on her mood and the toll it was taking on her. But ever since her second child was born, Karen had been complaining of physical symptoms that intensified with stress. For instance, she occasionally suffered from irritable bowel syndrome and pain in her joints. I referred her to a rheumatologist, who diagnosed Karen with fibromyalgia and recommended a course of treatment, including pain medication and bodywork.*

*It has been my experience that stress and psychological conflict sometimes play out on the physical level. Clients may experience their emotions physically, for example, instead of what we normally think of as emotionally. Consider the woman who told me she didn't feel anxious; she just had a nervous stomach, palpitations, difficulty catching her breath and chest pressure. I have seen clients who express their psychological stress somatically with headaches, backaches, stomachaches, generalized pain and even such symptoms as the inability to swallow or use their voices. There's considerable evidence that our mind and body are interrelated; doctors refer to illnesses that result from psychological factors like mental or emotional issues as psychogenic.*

*I always encourage clients to see their primary care physicians for medical checkups to rule out any physiological causes for their symptoms, because physical illnesses can be just what they seem. But bodily symptoms can also signify a psychological conflict a person is not ready to face or that something is not working in the person's life. In Karen's case, I had long suspected that her physical pains were a manifestation of her troubled relationship and conflicted feelings about her marriage and possibly trauma left over from her early years. However, people need to make these connections in their own time. I would never have recommended that Karen leave her husband, although I did repeatedly encourage her to attend couple's treatment with him. John refused. It was not until years later, when she finally realized that this relationship was unhealthy for her and she was strong enough to consider separating, that John finally relented and agreed to enter couple's therapy. By this time, though, it was hopeless and after two sessions with a marital therapist, he decided that treatment offered him nothing valuable and he terminated it.*

*It was not until she finally divorced John, after years of emotional abuse, that Karen's fibromyalgia improved to the point where she was sometimes pain free. Watching her transform into a healthy woman reinforced the notion that a healthy mind is intrinsic to maintaining a healthy body.*

*Karen's life has changed remarkably since I met her more than nine years ago, after the birth of her first child. I have watched her draw on an inner strength and a vast capacity for personal growth that has enabled her to grow profoundly and transform into an independent, confident, mature woman.*

*As with many clients I've observed, Karen's illness was a catalyst for change and tremendous inner growth. It was the significant turning point that provided motivation for her to explore personal issues, resolve past wounds and ultimately look for greater meaning in her life. As I have said repeatedly, postpartum depression is not the end of the story but often the beginning of an exploration. For Karen, it led to a metamorphosis that I believe would not have happened otherwise. It made her challenge her firmly held beliefs that she was inadequate, that her spouse was a healthy partner for her and that she had already moved beyond the pain of her abusive childhood. In challenging these beliefs, she was able to open up and reevaluate many of the relationships and conventions in her life. Today Karen is a much healthier person, more secure and capable of loving, intimate connections. She has begun a process of finding herself, healing the hurt child inside and becoming a happy woman.*

*This is a process you too can undertake. Explore yourself and utilize the postpartum experience you are going through to understand yourself more fully. Evaluate the past and how it has influenced you as well as your own beliefs and relationships. The knowledge and self-understanding you will gain can lead you from one of the most difficult periods in your life to becoming, like Karen has, the person you were meant to be.*

---

# CHAPTER 8

## *Principle I:*
## *Finding Ways to Heal*

When you're depressed, your ultimate challenge may seem to be finding a way to heal. Equally hard is finding a purpose for your illness and transforming whatever needs to be changed in your life—after all, something must not be working right or you wouldn't be suffering so. Contrary to accepted wisdom, postpartum depression is more than a hormonal or chemical imbalance. I'm not discounting the benefit that medication provides for some women. Being unbalanced hormonally or chemically can be part of the picture. However, it's only *part* of the picture. Even in mothers who have an imbalance, it's not the whole explanation. The reasons for this condition are complicated and vary from person to person. The one constant is that there's a lesson in it, even if that lesson is different for each woman. Once they accept that, they can stand back and see their difficulties as learning opportunities instead of the enemy, an alien that has overtaken their whole beings. It is then that they can make life changes and inspire themselves to recover and grow.

In an article by the renowned internist Lee Lipsenthal in the magazine *Holistic Primary Care*, Lipsenthal wrote about his observation of a friend suffering moderate depression: "We need to bear in mind that while pharmacotherapy can sometimes be life-saving in severe depression, it can also negate the possibility of personal growth, especially if the pharmacologic approach is used without psychotherapy or other introspective work." He pointed out that health and illness are profoundly influenced by cultural and commercial factors and that by relying solely on pharmaceuticals we may inadvertently decrease an individual's chance for spiritual and personal development. Thus, Dr. Lipsenthal concluded, even when it's appropriate to prescribe antidepressants, they should be used in conjunction with self-evaluative work and talk therapy.[1]

I, too, see depression as a chance to reevaluate one's life, to change goals and relationships in order to improve one's well-being.

You and your baby are undergoing parallel experiences: You are both birthing a new, growing self and you are both in a kind of infancy. It is not enough to watch your baby's development; *you* have to mature as well—personally, emotionally and spiritually.

In her book *The Second Journey: The Road Back to Yourself*, author Joan Anderson writes that "spiritual journeys begin with a 'call,' an irresistible pull to find our higher self." She describes a sacred restlessness that often initiates a quest "to wrest meaning from meaninglessness, find a revised sense of purpose, and create a new consciousness about life that depends more on fulfilling our inner needs than satisfying our outer desires."[2] Although Anderson focuses mostly on our middle years, it is my contention that these opportunities exist throughout our lives. Spiritual journeys often follow our darkest times, such as postpartum depression, when out of desperation we open up to a world of possibilities not previously considered.

Many books on postpartum depression are devoted to helping you understand the illness or heal your symptoms. These and other resources can be valuable for your recovery (refer to the compilation in appendix A). But the intent of this book is different. I want to inspire you, to give you hope and, ultimately, to alter your perception of postpartum depression. I'd like you to learn to view this difficult experience as an occasion to set out on a passage of your own. I know it's tough to imagine anything positive coming out of this hurt, but I assure you it's possible; it can happen despite the pain you're now feeling. This can be a time to reevaluate yourself and your life, to look at how you have been living and to find the ways you can live differently. Take the challenge and embrace growth.

I am not alone in seeing this as a time of transformation and purpose. The women whose stories I present agree that it was an experience that changed them in remarkable ways. This is an opportunity you do not want to pass up.

In the general population, women who experience postpartum depression are at higher risk of having another, often more severe episode with each subsequent pregnancy. Yet over the past several years, I have noticed that some of my clients do not suffer ensuing bouts. When mothers complete their treatment, I often recommend that if they become pregnant again or consider having another child, they should schedule a consultation to discuss PPD prevention and create a postpartum plan. Many of the women in these follow-up sessions report a completely different experience during their next pregnancies: They're asymptomatic. I evaluate them after delivery, but they don't need more treatment.

What changes for these women? Why don't they have another episode of postpartum depression? Is it something about the prevention session that alters their incidences of postpartum depression? Is it the monitoring or the postpartum planning or some combination? Though I can't answer unequivocally, I believe it's the life changes they have made that lower their risk. What I know is that something is different and many never suffer from this illness again.

I'm not trying to minimize postpartum depression. Nor am I suggesting you seek spiritual awareness, meditation or self-reflection in lieu of professional treatment. I strongly urge treatment from a licensed mental health provider. Until you have some symptom relief and clear thinking, it's unlikely you will be able to sort out your experience, particularly on your own.

It's essential that you take this illness seriously, which means including psychotherapy as a key ingredient in your recovery and sometimes taking medication, too. It's critical to work with a therapist who has had significant experience and, if possible, specialization with postpartum depression and anxiety. This could be a psychologist, psychiatrist, social worker, counselor or psychiatric nurse. You and your therapist should "fit," that is, you should feel a connection with this person, so you can be open and honest with her or him. After all, you both share the same goal: your recovery. I am not suggesting there is a quick fix, but you should see some progress after a few sessions. If you're not getting better through treatment, whether it's because the two of you don't fit or the treatment itself is ineffective, find another therapist. You have to take care of yourself and get well, even if it means starting over with someone new. Be persistent until you find a professional who can help you.

However, sometimes a lack of improvement is not a sign that the therapy is ineffective but that you need a combined treatment approach. This is often true among women with moderately severe to severe symptoms of postpartum depression or those who are not responding to therapy alone. Medication is best prescribed and managed by a psychiatrist, although your primary care physician or obstetrician-gynecologist also can do so. Finding a psychiatrist with expertise in perinatal issues is favorable. Furthermore, some women find it beneficial to participate in postpartum support groups as a way to share their experiences and get emotional help from others going through the same experiences. This can be a wonderful adjunct to therapy and medication, but it should not be used as a substitute for individual treatment.

Therapy, medication, support groups: All are important tools for getting healthy. Yet ultimately, they are only pieces of the puzzle.

If you look at recovery as just getting rid of symptoms, then those three components are adequate. But is adequate enough? Don't you want real wellness and optimal health? Of course! And that means personal growth. So you must consider the meaning that is attached to your illness. As discussed earlier, finding such a meaning or purpose in your experience will help you transform your life and develop beyond the point of symptom remission.

Over the years I have had numerous conversations with clients and friends about the wisdom of the body. It seems that at times we use our mind to fool ourselves into thinking everything is fine. Often clients come in and report that they "don't get it"; they do not understand why they are having panic attacks when everything in their lives is ideal. They say they love their jobs, their spouses are wonderful, they have everything they ever wanted. This reminds me of Jennifer, a client who insisted all was perfect and that she was married to the greatest and most supportive man. Despite this, her anxiety attacks happened only on the weekends or in the evenings after her children went to bed and particularly when she had the opportunity to be alone with her husband. However, no matter how much she tried to convince herself that her marriage was not the problem, the symptoms in her body told a different tale.

When there is an inconsistency between what our minds tell us and what our bodies display, our bodies are likely telling the true story. Sometimes when we are not ready to face a situation head-on, the body will develop a symptom that makes it evident there is a problem. The symptom, in turn, makes it almost impossible to ignore the underlying difficulty. In your own healing process, try to consider aspects of your life that are not working well for you. Could your body be trying to signal you about something you are resisting? Often it's difficult to admit these things to ourselves or even to be aware of them. Talking to a good therapist can frequently help you see your symptoms with fresh eyes and address those aspects of your life that are not working.

But first you must eliminate the depression. You need to find ways to heal. There are several strategies and concepts to consider which can help you get started on healing your postpartum depression.

## COPING STRATEGIES AND INTERVENTIONS TO HEAL DEPRESSION

Let's look more closely at some of the coping strategies and therapeutic interventions that I discuss with women in therapy sessions. Therapy is individualized, so not all of these strategies will be useful or appropriate for all women. But I hope you find some good ideas to use by yourself or with your own therapist. My suggestions are meant to be a starting point for healing and change. Keep in mind, too, that when I'm working with someone on an intervention, I can guide her with much greater breadth and depth than I can offer you here.

**Eat Healthy Foods and on a Regular Schedule:** It's important to keep your meals healthy. Be sure to eat complex carbohydrates and proteins and avoid eating simple sugars like those found in cookies, candy and cake. Eating sweets like these will cause sugar-insulin dysregulation, a condition associated with other physical disorders, like hypoglycemia. Plus, it has been found that eating junk food—that is, foods loaded with refined sugar—causes a sudden rise in insulin, followed by a sharp drop. These ups and downs, known as a sugar rollercoaster, can play havoc with your moods.

Besides watching *what* you eat, pay attention to *when* you eat. To keep your blood sugar stable and avoid mood swings, be sure to eat small amounts regularly, perhaps as often as once every three hours. Often my depressed or anxious clients admit that they have stopped eating, because they have no appetites. Even if you don't feel hungry, you should eat some small amount (perhaps a few almonds, a protein drink or half a pint of yogurt). If you have further questions about nutrition, consider contacting a nutritionist or a dietician.

**Exercise:** Regular exercise means working out at least three to five times a week. There is a lot of research promoting exercise for good mental health as well as improved cognitive ability and physical fitness. We also now know that exercise can combat depressed and anxious moods. In the *APA Monitor,* a publication of the American Psychological Association (the largest scientific and professional organization of psychologists in the United States), a lead article in the December 2011 issue is devoted to the link between exercise and mental health. Michael Otto, PhD, a professor of psychology at Boston University, is quoted as saying that "usually within five minutes after moderate exercise you get a mood-enhancement effect." Beyond these short-term effects, additional research is finding that physical activity can also alleviate long-term depression.[3]

In one study on the efficacy of exercise, James Blumenthal, PhD, a psychologist at Duke University, researched the connection between mood and exercise and found that for patients with major depressive disorder, the effect of exercise was comparable to that of antidepressants. In addition, he later found that people who had continued exercising had lower relapse rates.[4] Consider the effectiveness of adding exercise to your current wellness program or to antidepressant medications you may be taking. More recently, psychologists have begun to study the effect of exercise on decreasing anxiety and panic attacks. Although this area is still being explored, the results look promising, so get moving!

**Sleep More:** Try to go to bed earlier and mind your *sleep hygiene.* This term is used to refer to following healthy sleep guidelines to ensure you are well rested and alert. Don't stay up late (even if you are not sleepy) and cut out caffeine drinks and foods (coffee, green and black caffeinated teas, both hot and iced, and chocolate) in the afternoons and evenings. In addition, consider eliminating sugary foods late in the day, as they stimulate your brain and may make it difficult to relax at bedtime or may give you dreams that are bad or more intense. Other things can stimulate the brain, too, like watching television or using a computer (it's been suggested that the light emitted from the screen causes wakefulness). Be careful of drinking alcohol; though many people say drinking helps them relax, it can actually affect sleep architecture (the stages and cycles of sleep, such as REM) and, ultimately, sleep hygiene.

I know that having a baby makes it more challenging to get some sleep. Although these suggestions may be fine for some women, those who have infants or babies and, consequently, whose days and nights are mixed up may find themselves feeling frustrated over sleeplessness. For parents of newborns or babies who are not on any kind of regular sleep schedule, I recommend the book *On Becoming Babywise: Giving Your Infant the Gift of Nighttime Sleep* by Gary Ezzo and Robert Bucknam, MD. Many of my clients say reading this book was valuable in getting their babies into routines and on the way to becoming good sleepers. See if it helps you, too! Another resource that offers good suggestions and information about sleep is *Power Sleep: The Revolutionary Program That Prepares Your Mind for Peak Performance* by Dr. James B. Maas of Cornell University.

**Restrict Alcohol:** I've already touched upon alcohol use, but the subject warrants more attention. Despite the initial euphoria, this drug is a depressant. Over the years, I have noticed (and warned clients) that more than an occasional drink is not a good idea, particularly if you are on the verge of clinical depression. In my experience, alcohol can precipitate this illness. I believe that much depression seen in January is related more to the heavy alcohol use during the winter holidays than to the letdown of the holidays being over. If you're on antidepressants now, please realize that taking a depressant like alcohol is counterproductive and may even nullify the effectiveness of your medication.

**Cut Down on Caffeine:** As I mentioned earlier, keep your caffeine intake to a minimum, especially if you're prone to panic and anxiety. Read all the labels carefully on foods, beverages and over-the-counter drugs, because caffeine is included in some sodas, energy drinks and pain relievers. Also be aware that if the caffeine is naturally occurring, as it is in coffee, non-herbal tea and chocolate, you won't find it listed in the ingredients.

**Have Regular Physical Exams:** If you're struggling with depression or anxiety, it's important to rule out medical causes for your emotional distress. If you haven't seen your doctor recently, schedule a physical checkup and be sure to discuss all your emotional symptoms, even sleep and appetite problems, during the appointment. Often your physician will recommend a thorough blood workup, including a complete thyroid profile and a check for anemia; if your physician doesn't, suggest it yourself.

**Take Supplements:** While visiting your doctor, consider talking about adding a multivitamin to your daily regimen, plus two other health supplements in particular: vitamin D and omega-3. Considerable research indicates how important these supplements can be. Please remember: check with your physician before adding any supplement to your diet; this is essential if you are pregnant.

You may know vitamin D as the sunshine vitamin and certain foods, too, are natural sources: fish, fish-liver oils and egg yolks.

Other foods, like many dairy and grain products, may be fortified with it. Yet vitamin D deficiency is a global epidemic that's getting worse all the time. At conferences I've attended lately, it is a popular topic. "We estimate that vitamin D deficiency is the most common medical condition in the world," says Michael Holick, a professor of medicine, physiology and biophysics at the Boston University School of Medicine.[5]

People who spend very little time in the sun (or who cover up with lots of sunscreen—an otherwise good idea), who avoid dairy products (to which vitamin D is often added) or who eat strict vegetarian diets may be at higher risk for deficiency. Vitamin D is considered essential for strong bones and has long been associated with preventing rickets, a bone-softening disease affecting youths, but recent research has found that it plays a role in many other health conditions, like osteoporosis. Though symptoms of a deficiency can be subtle, all it takes to diagnose the condition is a simple blood test that checks the concentration of a substance called calcidiol. Ask your doctor about this screening.

As for omega-3 or fish oil, this is a fatty acid found in foods like walnuts, some fruits and vegetables and cold-water fish. It has been linked with a lower risk for heart disease and stroke and with the reduction of symptoms associated with hypertension, depression, attention deficit hyperactivity disorder, joint pain and rheumatoid problems. According to WebMD, it may also boost the immune system. Research is now finding that it may be helpful in combating postpartum depression as well. A pilot study conducted at the University of Arizona College of Medicine suggested positive preliminary results for the use of omega-3 in the prevention and treatment of postpartum depression. Although taking this supplement is not the solution for everyone, I encourage you to look into the benefits and discuss the possibility of adding an omega-3 supplement with your doctor.

**Increase Sunlight:** We all need sunlight. However, some people are so sensitive to the reduction of sunlight in the fall and winter months that they become depressed. These individuals are said to have seasonal affective disorder (SAD). There are a couple of ways to increase the amount of sunlight you get: You can take a walk outside at midday, when the sun is at its peak, or you can supplement your sunlight artificially. For the latter, try using a light box, a therapy lamp or full-spectrum lightbulbs (the clear ones seem to be better for this purpose than the frosted ones). Several manufacturers make full-spectrum bulbs and they're readily available in many stores and some health food stores as well as online and through catalogs.

**Set Small, Manageable Goals:** In recovering from postpartum depression, it can be useful to set up a few—say three—small daily goals for yourself. These can be things such as taking the baby outside or on an errand all by yourself, taking a shower, making yourself a nice lunch or calling a friend. This will help you feel like you've accomplished something positive during the day. It can also be a way to measure your progress in getting better. For instance, you might notice that it's becoming easier and easier to achieve these objectives. Keep pushing yourself a little beyond your comfort zone. (This is beneficial for everyone: If you keep doing what you've always done, you stop developing and growing and become stagnant.) *Within limits,* putting pressure on yourself to complete a task can make you feel better. Just don't try to do too much and exhaust yourself. For women who are compulsive list-makers, always measuring success by how much they get done, consider instead letting go of more and not measuring your worth by a to-do list.

**Enjoy Sex:** You are probably wondering how this could possibly help you if you are already exhausted, depressed and/or anxious. What new mother, especially one with postpartum illness, is thinking about her libido or how to get sex back into her life? You're probably thinking about getting sleep or time alone. But sex is important.

The strong correlation between staying sexually active and remaining physically healthy has been known for some time. Recent claims by sex researchers indicate that women who have sexual relations and experience orgasm feel improved mental health and decreased depression as well. Sex stimulates the body to secrete oxytocin—sometimes known as "the love hormone"—and various neurotransmitters or chemicals in the brain, all of which improve your sense of well-being and forge a mutual connection between you and your partner. Oxytocin plays an important role in childbirth, labor and breast-feeding and is largely responsible for bonding and attachment with your baby. A growing body of evidence including that by the Kinsey Institute suggests that it may also play a role in alleviating postpartum depression.[6] Make time for sex and it will help you and your partner feel better.

**Nurture Supportive Relationships:** One of the risk factors for postpartum depression is the lack of a support network. As I've indicated earlier, withdrawing from social relationships, including friends and family, has a negative effect on healing from depression. However, it's not uncommon for women struggling with depression or anxiety to avoid contact with others, even people with whom they're close. I suggest you push yourself a little and reach out to others. This may be a good time to join a support group or a new moms' group. Postpartum Support International is a good starting point; it offers a partial listing of support groups by location. (For more organizations that may be helpful, see appendix A, "Resources for Women, Families and Healthcare Providers.")

**Find Your Balance:** Renowned psychologist Sigmund Freud said that life is about the human need to love, work and play. This reminds me that we all seem to have an innate need for balance in our lives. Everyone probably knows someone whose lifestyle is "out of whack." The person may be overscheduled or just maintain a hectic pace, which eventually leads to feeling overwhelmed and anxious. Then there are those who have too little going on: They often seem lethargic, depressed, lacking interests and bored. They may *be* boring as well. While folks in the overactive and overextended group cannot seem to stop, people in the underactive group cannot seem to get going. (If you are a compulsive over-doer, I suggest reading the book *Overdoing It: How to Slow Down and Take Care of Yourself* by Bryan Robinson.) Both extremes are unhealthy and can lead to physical and mental problems. A better alternative is a balanced lifestyle, in which you recharge your battery by making time for friends, fun, exercise, healthy eating, creative interests and work you enjoy. Look over the list of coping strategies and interventions and you'll find that many of the topics I discuss can help put you on the path to a more balanced life.

**Pursue Creative Activities:** Eminent professor and psychologist Mihaly Csikszentmihalyi wrote an article for *American Psychologist* that grabbed my attention and introduced me to the importance of creative activity as an intervention in healing depression and increasing joyfulness. In his article, Csikszentmihalyi focuses on one dimension of happiness, which he coined *flow*. In the state of flow, he explains, a person is so fully absorbed or engaged in an activity that he or she is temporarily unaware of time and nothing else seems to matter. In his article in *American Psychologist*, he describes "a particular kind of experience that is so engrossing and enjoyable that it becomes 'autotelic,' that is, worth doing for its own sake."[7] Creative activities are typical examples of these kinds of experiences.

To learn more about the efficacy of creativity and flow, I attended a conference on creativity in therapy and began to integrate some of those ideas into my practice. Now, in addition to being more innovative with the interventions and tools I give my clients, I encourage women to find creative activities of their own to advance their recoveries. Surprisingly, this is therapeutic not only for the clients but for me, the healer, as well.

Too often we choose activities with a particular goal in mind (for example, we bake cookies not for the fun of it but to put them in the children's lunch bags or to sell at a fund-raiser). What I recommend is that you choose pursuits you enjoy so much that you'll forget your problems and your troubling thoughts for a while and just get in the "zone." It's all right to enjoy the goal, too, but the focus should be on the *process* or the act of doing the activity, which defines it as therapeutic and a flow experience. Some examples are baking, cooking, painting, sculpting, beading, weaving, quilting, knitting, playing an instrument, writing poetry or in a journal, singing or gardening.

To learn more about the experience of flow, you may want to read some of Mihaly Csikszentmihalyi's books: *Finding Flow: The Psychology of Engagement with Everyday Life*, *Creativity: Flow and the Psychology of Discovery and Invention* and *Flow: The Psychology of Optimal Experience.*

**Bring Humor into Your Life:** Have you ever heard that laughter is the best medicine? It may not be the only medicine for depression, but there are substantiated physical and mental health benefits from laughter and humor. Former *Saturday Review* editor Norman Cousins claimed to heal himself of a serious illness primarily with laughter and vitamins. When clients are clinically depressed, they often lose their senses of humor and stop finding things funny. The sound of a client's laughter is a positive beginning sign of recovery. It doesn't matter what tickles your funny bone—whether it's a popular romantic comedy movie or an old Marx Brothers' film. Consider, too, joke books, humorous authors, stand-up comedians, TV sitcoms and funny online videos.

**Establish Realistic Expectations and Leave Perfectionism Behind:** It's great that you want to be a good mother. But how good is good enough? Try to answer that question truthfully. Ask yourself, "Am I being realistic?"

Is there some ideal image in your mind of what a "perfect" mother should be? Is it something you read in a book, saw in a movie, were told by friends, observed in a shopping mall? Whatever the source, it's just a delusion, a mistaken notion. The idea of a perfect mother is not at all possible, so to think you can be this person is unrealistic. Most of us strive to be the best we can, but ask yourself, "How good is good enough?" Do you know any perfect mothers? Do you think your mom was perfect? I cannot think of one perfect mother, not among any of my friends, my family, my clients or myself. I do, however, know many moms who are trying their best, being conscientious and loving their children. I consider myself to be part of that group.

There is a difference between being conscientious and being a perfectionist. Being satisfied only with perfection, an impossible illusion, sets you up to be self-critical and disappointed or angry with yourself; it does not make you a better mother. It is likely to make you feel inadequate and to harm your self-esteem.

If you are struggling to be perfect, this may be the time to begin working on changing that irrational idea. You are not alone. There are many perfectionists out there. Here are a few of the many books that address this issue: *Too Perfect: When Being in Control Gets Out of Control* by Allan Mallinger, MD, and Jeannette DeWyze; *The Gifts of Imperfection: Let Go of Who You Think You're Supposed to Be and Embrace Who You Are* by Brene Brown; *How Good Do We Have to Be? A New Understanding of Guilt and Forgiveness* by Harold Kushner.

**Make Time to Care for Yourself:** We all need to take time for good self-care and we should not feel guilty about it. There has been much written about how a person can't take care of anyone else if she is not healthy herself. Would you go to a dentist who did not take care of his teeth? Would you trust a doctor who didn't take care of her health? Then why would you expect to be admired for neglecting and sacrificing yourself? Be a good role model to your children, friends and spouse: Treat yourself with respect and others will respect you and treat you well, too.

Airline representatives have been giving us this advice for years: In case of emergency, they always say, put on your own oxygen mask before trying to help others, such as your children. If you are oxygen-deprived and unable to function well, you will be little use to anyone else. But if you remain calm and clear-headed, you will be much more capable of assisting the people around you. It's the same principle with good self-care. If you attend to your own needs, you'll have more to offer your family and friends.

Good self-care involves following the coping strategies and interventions discussed in this chapter (plus any personal ones you may think of—say, taking a relaxing bath or getting a manicure). For more self-care ideas, read the blog Living Self-Care (http://livingselfcare.wordpress.com), which offers many inspiring suggestions and links to other sites. You can also sign up for the Living Self-Care Challenge, which helps to motivate women to practice self-care by "tweeting tips for inner peace and happiness" and awarding random prizes. A book which offers good additional tips is *What About Me? A Simple Guide to Self-Care in the 21st Century* by Stacey Glaesmann.

**Maintain a Structured Routine:** People appear to be programmed to live within cycles (hormonal cycles, seasonal cycles, lunar cycles, astrological cycles). There is even speculation that humans are affected by physical, emotional and intellectual cycles that begin at birth, a phenomenon known as biorhythms. We seem to respond favorably to the repetition of sequences of events, which gives life some measure of predictability and pattern. We impose these patterns on our children (e.g., wash your hands before a meal, eat breakfast upon rising, dress nicely before you leave for school, enjoy dessert *after* dinner, brush your teeth before bed) and these routines give children a sense of security. They know what is expected of them and, in a small way, what they can expect of others. It minimizes the turmoil and disorder of life.

In the same way, I think following a succession of activities on a daily basis can also reduce the chaos in adult lives. It certainly has helped me. You too may find it advantageous.

For my own self-care, I have found that I benefit from a structured daily routine. There are certainly times when I prefer to be spontaneous and have no structure (this can be fun—and healthy, too). However, there's a benefit to keeping a rhythm to your life, as long as you stay flexible. Everyone needs to find the schedule that works best for her.

As a rule, I don't keep a schedule on weekends. I try to exercise, see films and spend time with loved ones. I indulge myself as much as possible, beginning with sleeping late. I like to vary the activities I enjoy on these days: dining in fine restaurants, going to the movies, taking day trips to museums, shopping, hanging out with friends, listening to live music at clubs, dancing or watching independent films.

I have found that having a daily routine or schedule has a definite, positive effect. I've suggested the practice to many of my clients and many report that it's had a favorable effect on their energy levels and moods. Their babies are also happier on a regular schedule of sleeping, eating and waking. Having structure and a routine is often very helpful for children as well as infants. Some children who are prone to hyperactivity seem to have more problems with unstructured activity, such as free time, school recess and unscheduled breaks.

**Change Your Thoughts to Change Your Mood:** If you're feeling depressed or anxious, there are two ways you can change your mood yourself: take an action/make a change in your behavior or alter your thoughts.

Some examples of taking action are exercising, doing something that distracts you and treating yourself to an activity you enjoy, such as knitting, listening to music or gardening. When you take action, you shift your mood (see the next section, "Take Action with Effort-Driven Rewards," for why this is true).

The other way to change your mood is to change what you are thinking. Psychologists say that thought and mood go hand in hand, like partners. Think angry thoughts and you'll feel angry. Think frightening or anxious thoughts, you'll feel anxious. You will never think angry thoughts and feel contentment and love or think frightening thoughts and feel relaxed and happy. If you do not like how you are feeling, change your thoughts and your feelings will change, too.

Identify what you are thinking. Unfortunately, you're not always aware of your thoughts; sometimes it's easier to know how you feel than what you're thinking. But those feelings can provide a clue to your thoughts. Try writing down your feelings and then the thoughts that make you feel this way. For example, let's say you're sitting alone at a coffee shop when you notice an acquaintance at a nearby table. As you try to get his attention, he continues to talk to the woman with whom he's sitting. Suddenly you feel hurt, angry and snubbed. These are the feelings you'd write down. What are the thoughts you're telling yourself? Maybe: *He's embarrassed to admit he knows me. How dare he!* This is followed by a host of other thoughts, such as, *He's never liked me. He always thinks he is better than me. He's an arrogant jerk.* Write these thoughts next to your feelings.

The next step is the most important: Consider your thoughts objectively to determine if they're rational. In this example, once you become aware of how your thoughts are giving rise to angry feelings, you could ask yourself questions such as, *What proof do I have that any of this is true? How do I know that what I'm thinking is correct? What's the likelihood that he's just absorbed in conversation and doesn't notice me?* Try to reason with yourself and look for evidence that what you think is actually true. Can you actually know from the situation that he's embarrassed to admit he knows you? Or that he thinks he's better than you? If in fact it *is* true—if your acquaintance *is* ignoring you and thinks he's better than you—then you have to accept it and perhaps you have a right to feel annoyed. This technique is not about lying to yourself or fooling yourself but about being rational and not inventing interpretations that in turn affect your mood.

Now, perhaps the waiter brings him some soup. At that moment your acquaintance looks up and, seeing you for the first time, smiles and waves. He calls out your name and asks how you're doing. Now you're filled with new thoughts: *I was wrong about him. He's really nice. I shouldn't jump to conclusions.* Stop and think about how you feel. My guess is much happier.

People tend to have certain patterns of distorted thinking. Psychologists have identified ten common cognitive distortions: all-or-nothing thinking, overgeneralization, mental filter, jumping to conclusions, disqualifying the positive, magnification or minimization, emotional reasoning, "should" statements, labeling and mislabeling and personalization. Most people use more than one of these, but we each seem to have our favorites. Try to identify which distortions you typically fall back on. Then work on changing your pattern.

It's a lot easier to use this approach within a therapy session, where you have a guide who can draw on real-life examples from your own thoughts and mood states to help you alter automatic, distorted thinking. But this simplified version of the technique can be effective when you use it on your own.

For more information on changing your thinking and mood, I suggest *Feeling Good: The New Mood Therapy* by David Burns, MD.

Additionally, there is a variety of workbooks, tapes and programs available to help you add this cognitive or cognitive-behavioral approach to the exercises you can do. It's only one of many methods therapists employ to help you work on changing your moods. Each therapeutic orientation has something valuable to offer and many therapists integrate several modalities.

**Take Action with Effort-Driven Rewards:** Reading about brain science, neuroscience and the ways the brain can heal itself can give you important information on utilizing your own powers to heal. In her book *Lifting Depression: A Neuroscientist's Hands-On Approach to Activating Your Brain's Healing Power,* author Kelly Lambert, PhD, reveals that she suffered from clinical depression following the death of her mother. *Lifting Depression* explains how she healed herself by using action to jump-start her brain's accumbens-striatal-cortical network, also known as the effort-driven rewards circuit. Lambert used vacuuming as her activity to better mental health. As she explains in her book, to protect ourselves from depression or to treat the condition we need to find a meaningful physical activity that requires effort, restores some control over our environment and helps reactivate this system in the brain, which she suggests is "a prime suspect for the neuroanatomical circuit underlying the symptoms associated with depression." The task must involve using your hands, she adds. Other examples might include cooking, knitting a sweater, scrapbooking or gardening.[8]

**Relieve Trauma with Eye Movement Desensitization and Reprocessing (EMDR):** When I was working at the Veterans Administration Medical Center inpatient Stress Disorder Treatment Unit, a program that provides intensive hospitalization to veterans who have been diagnosed with post-traumatic stress disorder (PTSD) as a result of combat experience, the lead psychologist was concerned about the rate of return, known as the recidivism rate, for treatment. He questioned the effectiveness of current therapeutic interventions since veterans continued to return repeatedly for treatment.

He arranged with the medical administration to bring a clinical psychologist, Francine Shapiro, PhD, from the Mental Research Institute in California, to train the VA psychologists, social workers and psychiatrists in a new technique called eye movement desensitization and reprocessing (EMDR). Dr. Shapiro had found that the use of eye movements was incredibly effective in relieving the symptoms of PTSD and began researching its use with both veterans and others, such as victims of rape, accidents, physical and sexual abuse and other trauma. She found amazing results and EMDR has become an established method for treating PTSD as well as offering applications for treatment of other anxiety disorders and mental health problems. EMDR is taught and used both domestically and internationally as a legitimate therapeutic technique.

EMDR "accelerates the treatment of a wide range of pathologies and self-esteem issues related to disturbing events and present life conditions...the method is capable of a rapid desensitization of traumatic memories, including a cognitive restructuring and a significant reduction of client symptoms (e.g., emotional distress, intrusive thoughts, flashbacks and nightmares)," according to the training materials and manuals.[9]

EMDR can be used along with other therapeutic practices and coping strategies; many clinicians consider it one of many therapy tools and incorporate it into an eclectic assortment of interventions that they can utilize with clients, as appropriate. Be aware that while some clients really benefit from this procedure, it is up to the discretion of your own therapist if this would be a useful and beneficial intervention to include in your individualized treatment plan.

I began using this technique with many of the veterans with whom I was working and, over the past twenty years, I have continued to use EMDR with my clients who have post-traumatic stress disorder in addition to the postpartum illness for which they have sought treatment. I find it can be quite effective with many clients who have past histories that include trauma that may pre-date their PPD; for example, a client who was a victim of child abuse. In addition, I find that the method can be quite successful in treating clients who have birth trauma, have perinatal loss or are traumatized by the intensity of their own postpartum episode. This can occur with a subsequent pregnancy, in which a woman is so frightened after having postpartum depression previously that she has significant symptoms of anxiety, agitation, nightmares, worry and intrusive memories which intensify as she gets closer to the date for delivery of her baby.

Please note: EMDR is not a technique that you can do on your own; it must be used by a trained clinician who has attended and been certified through the EMDR Institute, Inc.

**Listen to Music to Soothe Your Soul:** Music can lift you up, inspire you and alter your mood. In his article "Music Soothes the Soul," New York psychotherapist Mark Sichel writes, "singing, listening, and creating music of any kind will provide an immediate biological and psychological benefit for everyone. In fact, music can be a salvation and antidote to most psychological challenges."[10] According to "Music and Song: the Sounds of Hope?" in *Positive Psychology News Daily*, research findings report "the immediate psychological and medical benefits of music: increased happiness, less stress, reduced depression symptoms, greater autonomy, and increased competence, hope, and optimism."[11]

I find music can be a wonderful tool for clients and it's one I highly recommend to lift the blues. Certain melodies can revitalize you after a long day or can calm you when you're feeling anxious. Turn on your radio, play a CD or use an online streaming music service to listen to some smooth jazz, lounge, new age, ambient or nature sounds. I choose music selections that reflect my mood or the mood I wish to have.

**Surround Yourself with Inspiration:** To improve mood, it's helpful to connect to sources of inspiration, which can come from virtually anywhere. We draw energy from people around us, so choose friends who are upbeat and encouraging. Try to spend less time with relatives and acquaintances who whine and complain, tend to look at the negative side of life, view themselves as victims, drain your energy or just plain bring you down.

You can also raise your mood by watching inspirational films, listening to moving music, reading uplifting books or repeating or surrounding yourself with positive affirmations. Consider buying affirmation cards or desk calendars or write down your own.

**Use Social Networking Sites to Connect and Create:** You can use social networking sites to get in touch with old friends, classmates and colleagues. This can be helpful in expanding your support network and feeling less alienated. (Be sure to set your privacy settings so your photos and comments are not public.) Another way to connect to others—while being creative, too—is to blog. Also consider following other people's blogs and posting responses to their entries (be sure to visit my blog at http://post-postpartumdepressionblog.com).

**Share and Help Others:** Have you noticed that when you are depressed or going through a difficult period you become self-absorbed? It's hard to think of others when you're stuck in your own suffering. No one means to be self-centered but pain seems to demand attention. During such times, you may have trouble empathizing with other people or reaching out to them. You can get stuck in a web of self-pity and turn into an internally focused victim. All of this is quite typical and a symptom of depression.

There are many tools to use when you're struggling with depression, but one of the best ways to help yourself is to reach out and help someone else. This may feel like the last thing you want to do, yet it really can shift your myopic focus. Do you know someone less fortunate who could use some help? Have you considered doing volunteer work? Can you offer to help a friend or relative? As you share your time and talents, the person you're helping starts to feel better—and so do you!

Another way to share and help others is to "pay it forward." It works like this: Instead of paying someone back for a kindness, you repay the good deed by paying it *forward* to three new people, that is, by doing something nice for three others. One person helps another, who helps another and another and another and so on, the positive effect multiplying exponentially. Sometimes we feel powerless to change ourselves or our world. This ingenious practice offers a simple way to create a chain reaction of change. As the Pay It Forward Foundation (http://payitforwardfoundation.org) proclaims in its motto, "one act of kindness can change everything."

**Practice Mindfulness:** This concept, originally from Buddhist meditation, means living fully in the present moment. Practicing mindfulness can be effective in combating depression, anxiety and obsessive thinking. Jon Kabat-Zinn, a clinical psychologist and the director of both the Stress Reduction Clinic and the University of Massachusetts Medical Center, helped bring mindfulness meditation and thinking to Western life and therapy. As Kabat-Zinn writes in his book *Wherever You Go, There You Are: Mindfulness Meditation in Everyday Life*, "to find our way, we will need to pay more attention to this moment. It is the only time that we have in which to live, grow, feel and change."[12] That is precisely what mindfulness is about.

Often my clients (my friends and relatives, too) say they have negative thoughts that make them feel depressed or anxious. This is quite common; at times we all find ourselves worrying about something that hasn't even happened. We read that college tuitions are going up and we wonder, *What if I don't have enough money to send my daughter to college?* Or we obsess, *What if I get sick and can't work and have no way to support myself and my family?* We go on and on, ruminating over distressing hypotheticals. (You can usually spot the catastrophic thoughts by the telltale "what if..." at the beginning.)

Mindfulness is the antidote to these upsetting future-oriented musings as well as the remedy for regrets ("If only I had/hadn't..."). As Kabat-Zinn writes, "It often seems as if we are preoccupied with the past, with what has already happened, or with a future that hasn't arrived yet." Instead, he admonishes, we should feel the present moment fully.[13]

I recommend reading the magazine *Mindful*, which focuses on the benefits of mindfulness and ways to experience the power and pleasure of living in the present. Also, seek books and inspirational

CDs by authors like Kabat-Zinn and Eckhart Tolle that can help you achieve the desired changes in your thinking.

---

### Marla's Story

*One day I received a distraught phone call from a woman I'd known for years but saw as a client only periodically for maintenance. We'd had a therapy session just the week before, so I was surprised to hear from her again so soon. Years earlier, Marla had struggled with postpartum depression, for which she had taken antidepressant medication and gone to regular weekly therapy sessions. The combination of treatments improved her postpartum depression and panic symptoms, which eventually remitted. Feeling like her old self, she resumed life as a full-time teacher and the primary parent of two young children. We kept in contact, scheduling a few sessions each year.*

*Eventually, Marla decided that she'd been well for so long that, with the help of her psychiatrist, she could taper off the medication. In the months that followed, she did fine. She continued to see me, although our appointments became less regular. I took it as a sign that she was doing well and no longer needed the support of a therapeutic relationship.*

*However, one day she called to tell me that things were starting to get to her; she felt on the verge of a panic attack. I set up an appointment to see her, but when Marla came in she said she was feeling better. Since Christmas was approaching, she attributed the anxiety to the pressure of the holiday, the children being home from school and all the rushing around. We scheduled another session, with the caveat that should she notice any other panic symptoms or increasing anxiety, she would let me know right away.*

*Not long after the holiday, Marla called again and reported that her anxiety had gotten worse since Christmastime. For two days she hadn't been able to go to work but instead had been worrying about the future, fearing she wouldn't have enough money to keep up with inflation and fretting about the health of her aging parents. She had not eaten since the day before and had experienced a panic attack which left her feeling drained, frightened and hopeless.*

*I listened to Marla and we discussed several steps she could take to feel better. The first was to eat a healthy snack every two or three hours, whether or not she felt hungry. She confessed that she had been indulging in unhealthy, sugary foods in the weeks surrounding Christmas. I felt this may have contributed to her recent mood fluctuations. She also told me that she rarely got any exercise and that her office was lit with fluorescent lights. This led me to my second recommendation: that she take a walk outdoors midday, which would provide mood-elevating exercise and exposure to sunlight at the same time.*

*I asked about her alcohol use, since people often celebrate the holidays with parties and drinking. She admitted she had been imbibing a lot more than usual during December. We discussed the likelihood that this had contributed to her anxiety and low moods. She also disclosed that she had been going to bed later than usual and not sleeping well (possibly because of her increased alcohol use).*

*My final recommendation was that she make an appointment with her physician for a physical exam, including a check of her thyroid and vitamin D levels and a discussion about the benefits of taking supplements like vitamin D and omega-3. Marla seemed relieved by my suggestions. We ended the conversation by setting up an appointment for the following week.*

---

## DISCOVER WAYS TO HEAL

There is no how-to manual on recovering from postpartum depression and, like Marla, each woman must discover her own path. Look to your therapist, spouse, family and friends for help and support. Consider joining a group of other mothers who are going through the same experience. And consider the benefits of taking medication prescribed by a psychiatrist or other physician who's treating you and is in a position to evaluate your condition. Some people feel ashamed to take medication, see a therapist or even talk to a friend about their postpartum experience. Remember, there is no shame in seeking help in order to get better.

Next I offer some suggestions to get you thinking about ways you can lift your mood and apply self-care. My hope is that these ideas—beyond therapy, medication and support groups—will inspire you to get creative about your own recovery process. Maintaining your spirit on the difficult journey to health and personal meaning is imperative in order to create a more fulfilling future.

### Creative Ways to Help You Heal

- Watch uplifting movies.
- Read inspiring books.
- Enjoy poems and quotations that lend insight.
- Listen to soothing music.
- Go to a museum or gallery to view art you like in a tranquil setting.
- Spend time in natural surroundings.
- Indulge in creative activities that bring you pleasure.
- Dance.
- Exercise regularly.
- Practice yoga and/or meditation.
- Try to be mindful and present in the moment.
- "Pamper" yourself with some relaxation.
- Keep a personal journal.
- Make alone time for yourself.

- Spend time with your spouse or partner without the baby.
- Get together with supportive friends and family members.

Spend time writing down your own ideas to add to the list of creative ways to lift your mood and find healing. Taking care of yourself—and taking the time to do it—is not selfish. It's your duty to yourself!

---

## IN HER OWN WORDS: RUTH'S STORY

*I stopped using birth control at age thirty-four. I thought I would conceive the first time I had sex after that. In fact, I thought I felt myself conceive right then and there. So began my years-long journey to discover that I wouldn't get pregnant without some help. A friend of mine who'd had a baby after fertility treatments told me, it's not how you drive…it's how you arrive. This was the best advice I ever heard. Once you have your baby in your arms, it doesn't matter how it all came about. You have your child and family.*

*I began fertility treatments and shortly afterward I became pregnant with my daughter. Her birth was the most beautiful, magnificent time in my life and continues to be every day. Yet looking back on it, I'm sure I didn't feel very good physically, although I didn't realize it then. Having my baby was such a miracle that I wasn't aware of all my hormonal changes. I wanted to have more children, but I wasn't sure how long it would take to get pregnant again. So when my daughter was six months old, I underwent more fertility treatments and began trying again. Soon I was pregnant with my second child.*

*To break the news to my parents and sisters, I had a large sheet cake made with a baby carriage on it and a line that read "Girl or Boy, Each a Joy!" Since I'd just had a successful full-term pregnancy and a gorgeous baby, I told everyone about our second pregnancy, even though it had been only a week since I found out myself. Whenever I was driving around with my daughter, in my mind there were three of us in the car already. But three months into my pregnancy, I miscarried and descended into a place sadder and more difficult than I had ever imagined.*

*It seemed like a great miracle, then, when I got pregnant once more a short while later, this time with my beautiful son. What I remember the most after his birth, however, is knowing that I wasn't right emotionally. Still, the great joy I had with my babies kept me moving forward even when I didn't feel I could manage it physically. It felt so strange: I was filled with joy over my children and yet felt horrible and sad about myself and my future. This just can't be, I thought. I must get help and I must get help now.*

*Around that time, I saw a flyer for a postpartum group. I was in such dire straits that I called the therapist leading the group so I could see her one-on-one. I couldn't believe how lucky I was to have come across this leaflet and to have found someone who knew what I was going through. Maybe she could help me understand what was happening to me and what to do about it.*

*Because I had this amazing, incredible family that I had waited my whole life for, I kept telling myself that what didn't kill me made me stronger. I truly knew this and felt it on a physical and emotional level. It didn't make sense that I was so sad.*

*Meeting my therapist and having her support and understanding, listening to her share her own experiences, gave me the lifeline I needed. It gave me something to hang on to—the hope that maybe, just maybe, I would be a whole person again and the joyful mom that I'd always dreamed of being.*

*Through my hardest days and dreadful emotions I used every ounce of energy I had left to be loving and happy with my babies. While they were napping and after they went to bed at night, I became a total zombie, saving up enough energy to be with them when they woke. Everything I did was from sheer force of will to sustain myself as a mother. How could this be? My therapist's guidance helped me understand the emotional challenges of being a mom and the many physical changes I was experiencing, too. I realized that even though I was thrilled to have my children, my hormones were making me depressed. This shift in my body was making it more difficult to function. My therapist also suggested seeing a psychiatrist for medications that could rebalance my chemistry and help me feel better physically so I could regain the joy in my life.*

*Today my children are ten and eight. I have faced many challenges, but all of them have made me stronger and more self-assured and have let me know great joy. Through my great pain has come great joy! Joy that I had someone in my corner to understand me and help me understand motherhood and the chemical changes it can bring. Joy that I don't feel a dark cloud over my head and that my body has regained a sense of balance. Joy that I can navigate my emotions even if I'm feeling stress and that I understand more and more each day how to manage. Joy that I am a better mother, wife and person, that I now can say I know what it feels like to be looking back on the fog of postpartum depression. I feel the sun shining and I can feel real joy!*

*Working with my therapist has given me insight and tremendous strength. She has taught me that even though something may feel wrong right now or even though you don't know how a situation will turn out, everything could be different tomorrow, next month or a year from today. That has given me the courage to know on the deepest level that anything is possible and that I can feel better. As Dr. Feingold says, the story is just unfolding. We don't know what situations will come up and change everything in the future. I have had many of those situations and will continue to have them.*

*It is with great joy that I look back on my path of postpartum depression. I have learned to be loving and kind to myself even when I don't know when the outcome of a situation will reveal itself. Thankfully, I received the help I needed. I recall my therapist telling me, "Of course you can swim across a freezing cold lake. But wouldn't it be nicer to get some help and take a boat?" I am so thrilled that I listened.*

---

Ruth's story is an example of a woman who desired to have a child so badly that she didn't take the time to heal and grieve her losses, which included a miscarriage and the loss of natural conception as well as the added stress of fertility treatments. The hormonal ups and downs along with conflicting emotions of simultaneous joy and grief can create a confusing state for a new mom.

Our therapeutic work allowed Ruth to process and mourn her losses while understanding and accepting the reason for her extreme array of emotions. In addition to various cognitive-behavioral interventions to help with depression, we used an insight-oriented approach to explore unresolved family issues. As Ruth grieved her immediate past losses, she also began to deal with strong feelings and remnants from her early years growing up with a mood-disordered mom who had struggled with depression and addictions to alcohol and other sedatives.

She and I are pleased at her new understanding and insight into the past as well as the strength she has gained now to progress and build a fulfilling family life.

# CHAPTER 9

## *Principle II:* *The Power of Hope and Inspiration*

Gaining hope that you will recover and then maintaining faith in that belief is the next step toward recovery from postpartum depression. Losing hope may put you at risk of contemplating the desire to end your life. Hope is a subject that resonates well in people. Take, for instance, Viktor Frankl's landmark book *Man's Search for Meaning*, in which the concentration camp survivor describes what he endured in World War II and discusses the need to find meaning in our experiences. Frankl identifies the drive toward having meaning in one's life as the primary motivation in humans. A survey by the Library of Congress in conjunction with the Book-of-the-Month Club found Frankl's slim volume to be one of the ten most influential books. By the time of his death, Frankl's book had sold twelve million copies in twenty-four languages. Frankl writes that what was basic to his and the other prisoners' survival was to find a reason to live—in other words, to have faith or hope that their hellish situation would eventually end. Those prisoners had to maintain some vision of the future or they were doomed. So do those who suffer postpartum depression.

This level of faith is what allows you to persevere even on bad days and to continue struggling for health. As I tell my clients, it's a road with twists and turns, but in the end we will figure it out together and you will cross that finish line to complete recovery.

It takes a great deal of strength and trust to accept this possibility in light of the negative thinking that accompanies postpartum depression.

This is often the greatest challenge: to convince a new client—someone so hopeless—to have faith once again and to trust me. Perhaps the fact that I myself went through the illness and recovered gives new clients hope.

There is power in what we believe. Isn't that what faith is all about, believing in something you cannot see? In Hebrews 1:1, the Bible states, "Faith is being sure of what we hope for and certain of what we can't see." And Martin Luther King Jr. said, "Faith is taking the first step even when you don't see the whole staircase."

When struggling with a physical or emotional problem, we are often told to have faith. Why is it so important? We must believe in our doctors or we won't follow their instructions; we may even stop seeing some physicians. We must have faith in the possibility of recovery or we'll give up in despair and become hopeless.

On a more concrete level, psychologists know that what we believe to be true influences us. There are even "laws" to describe some of these effects: self-fulfilling prophecy (in which something becomes true by virtue of our expecting it to happen) and interpersonal expectancy (which holds that people are more motivated when they believe they can achieve a goal based on others' optimistic expectations of them). Even in scientific research, we account for such biases and try to eliminate them by conducting double-blind studies. (Neither the subjects nor the researchers know who is in which test group and thus cannot be influenced by their expectations of the outcome.)

We see this not only in science but also in everyday life. Think about how you are shaped by information you read. Let's say you are a teacher and have a new student joining your class. You read the student's educational file, including comments from past teachers. What if it says this child is a troublemaker and disruptive? How will this influence you when you meet the student at school the next day? Will you be "on guard" and prepared to let the youngster know from the get-go that you're not going to put up with any funny business? Will you respond differently if you read instead that this is someone bright, gifted and well-liked by the staff and other students? Will you be more open, more receptive, perhaps more welcoming? As much as we like to think we're above this kind of reaction, prior knowledge affects us all.

However, it's not only what we read that influences us. Consider what happens when a teacher overhears others talking about a student in the teachers' lounge or when children talk about each other. When I worked at a public school I learned about an adolescent girl who had made an attempt on her own life after some classmates spread damaging rumors about her. We are all concerned about our "reputations." Apparently, the disapproval of her peers in her small, conservative, rural hometown was too painful for this girl to handle.

As a school psychologist, I evaluated students by observing them in the classroom, gathering information from their teachers and parents and testing them. Then I came up with conclusions to pass along to the staff for educational planning. It was always my practice to meet and test the children first and look at the results "blind," without talking to others or reading the school records. That way I could view the students without prejudice and not be influenced by what people thought or said about them. I think it gave me a truer, less biased picture. Even today, when I meet a new client who has visited another mental health provider, I like to make my own assessment before contacting the other professional for information; it reduces the effect the other therapist might have on my thinking and opinions.

There are many ways in which we're influenced by the information to which we have access. When we read a newspaper or news Web site and when we view images there, our ideas and emotions are affected. Imagine seeing a picture of a teenager hurt and bleeding in a war-torn region. Imagine how compassionate you might feel. Now suppose you read that the boy had just thrown a grenade at an outdoor market, killing dozens of innocent people. Would that change your reaction? What if the writer had his own bias? What if you later read a more detailed story by another journalist, who claimed the boy had been distraught over the loss of his family during an air force attack? The point is not that you can't trust anything you read or see but that we are influenced by many factors that alter the way we perceive things.

The film *What the Bleep Do We Know!?* includes a fascinating and relevant anecdote. When Columbus sailed for the New World, the native people of the West Indies, where he first landed, looked out at the water but could not "see" his ship. They saw the waves and the influence of the ship in the water, but because they had no mental concept of a ship, they were unable to perceive it. Imagine that! Apparently, it was not until a well-respected shaman saw the vessel and described it to them that they suddenly could distinguish it, too.

One psychology experiment by Daniel Simons and Christopher Chabris involves a video clip of several adults playing basketball. At the beginning of the clip, the viewer is instructed to count how many times the people dressed in white pass the ball. In the video, half a dozen men and women wearing either black or white T-shirts circle about and pass a basketball. After a few seconds, the activity stops and the narrator gives the correct answer. Then he adds, "But did you notice the gorilla?" *What gorilla?* I wondered the first time I watched it. The video quickly "rewinds" the scene and replays it. The second time, I saw that while the group plays, someone in a gorilla costume walks across the floor, pauses in the middle of the players, turns to face the camera and even beats his chest before continuing to saunter through the game. How had I failed to perceive this the first time? It's interesting that when the same video was shown at a psychology department meeting about a year after my initial viewing, I noticed the gorilla right away, though most of the staff who had not previously seen the film succumbed to selective attention just as I had done at first.

Psychologists know that what people think and their attitudes and beliefs influence their feelings. This is the basic tenet of cognitive-behavioral psychology. In this therapeutic approach, psychologists work with clients to change their ideas in order to change their feelings. It's effective with both depressed and anxious clients and is particularly useful in helping them dispute and alter their irrational beliefs and substitute sounder ones.

However, what if our thoughts and beliefs affect not only our feelings but also the events in our life? Is that possible? Some spiritual thinkers, including Rhonda Byrne, author of the popular book

*The Secret,* talk about a natural precept in the universe known as the Law of Attraction. This holds that our very thoughts have a type of magnetic force and a power that shapes not only ourselves (as psychologists have long claimed) but also, more importantly, the whole chain of events in the universe. We manifest our own destinies, because our minds create the phenomena that become the stuff of our lives.

In psychology, there is a growing body of evidence that supports the healing effect of faith, in particular an article by Jeff Levin, PhD, MPH, titled "How Faith Heals: A Theoretical Model" in *Explore: The Journal of Science and Healing.*

How does all this relate to recovery from postpartum depression? If you know that your thoughts have the power to transform your feelings and even what happens in your life, perhaps the thought that you will get well has the power to speed recovery. And having faith in that knowledge even when it feels most difficult has tremendous power.

Faith can keep you from feeling despair and hopelessness and it can be the difference between the client who contemplates suicide and the one who does not. If you know that your depression is finite and will go away in time, you might feel better already, more encouraged. Maybe faith can help you take this negative experience and turn it around, creating something positive and life-changing in its place. How do you get that level of faith? Is there a way to boost it?

Imagine how much better you would feel if you had faith in your recovery. Regardless of what you believe, psychologists know that the life-affirming thoughts associated with faith are advantageous. Take the challenge and increase your level of hope and faith. The effects could benefit your health, your state of mind and the realization of your goals.

### Ways to Increase Hope and Faith

- Surround yourself with positive affirmations. You can buy ready-made cards by authors like Louise Hay and Marianne Williamson or purchase smartphone apps like

Hay's "I Can Do It" calendar, which offers a different cheerful message every day. Better yet, write your own!

- Read upbeat, inspirational books and magazines, such as the bimonthly *Spirituality & Health*.
- Listen to CDs and podcasts that offer life-affirming messages.
- Watch inspirational films. Look into a DVD club like Spiritual Cinema Circle.
- Start a gratitude journal. Happy Tapper (http://happytapper.com) makes a smartphone app for one. Or, to get ideas about creating one yourself, visit http://spiritualityhealth.com/soul-body/practice/boost-and-share-your-gratitude.
- Attend an uplifting service at your church, synagogue or mosque.
- Practice yoga, meditate or listen to an inspirational lecture.
- Join a happiness project or begin one yourself. As an example, see Gretchen Rubin's book *The Happiness Project* and her Web site http://happiness-project.com.
- Come up with and write down five personal ways to boost hope and inspiration in your life.

---

## In Her Own Words: Ellen's Story

*For as long as I can remember, I dreamed of becoming a mom. I love children and I was excited to be able to demonstrate unconditional love to another person. I couldn't wait for the opportunity to teach young people about life and love. Motherhood had become a career goal. Although I was determined to complete my college education and graduate with a degree in pharmacy, the position of mom was always number one on my list of life goals. So after I graduated from university, I bought my first car, packed up my stuff and headed east for the city. I was young, single, educated and successful. My future seemed extremely bright.*

*But I was sad; I didn't like being single. I wanted to start a family—right away. I was twenty-four years old and I felt like my biological clock was ticking. Within a few years I was married and just three months after my wedding I was pregnant. To confirm my pregnancy, I bought about ten home testing kits. Since they were double packs, I ended up with twenty little plus signs. Life was good. My dreams were coming true!*

*My pregnancy was uncomplicated and uneventful. I felt wonderful, both physically and emotionally—no morning sickness or major mood swings and I could eat as much as I wanted. At least, that was what I thought at the time. Eating became overeating and I really packed on the pounds. My slender figure was no longer a part of my identity. The extra weight I gained probably didn't help my postpartum well-being. But I loved being pregnant and getting lots of attention and pampering from everyone. I felt as if I had done something no other woman had achieved. It felt surreal.*

*Then reality hit. My water broke in the early hours of a spring morning while I was asleep. It sounded just like the cork popping on a bottle of champagne. My husband rushed me to the hospital and we barely made it before our daughter's arrival. She was determined to enter the world quickly. There wasn't enough time for an epidural or even a shot of meperidine. About five minutes of pushing and she was born, our sweet baby girl. All of this happened within roughly two hours of the initial "cork-popping." For me, childbirth was excruciating but, thankfully, fast.*

*A couple of hours after delivery, our pediatrician said he wanted a neonatalogist to examine our baby, but he wasn't direct with us about why. As it turns out, he had noticed some "anomalies" he couldn't explain and thought they might signal Down syndrome. The specialist who examined our daughter concluded she was fine, but he ran some laboratory tests just to be sure. Unfortunately, those results would not be available for two weeks! So there I was, coming home from the hospital with my beautiful baby girl but worrying constantly about what the tests would show. Finally it was confirmed that my daughter was normal, but the whole scenario triggered so much anxiety that only seemed to get worse as time went on.*

*I became increasingly sad, depressed, anxious and agitated during my first few months postpartum. I could not sleep, so I spent the nights housecleaning compulsively while my husband and baby slept (I was fortunate to have a child who slept through the night at six weeks). Then in the daytime I was exhausted, which made my symptoms worse. Finally, at a low point, I broke down crying and screaming in front of my husband; I was completely out of control.*

*He didn't know what to do. But thankfully I had enough strength to recognize that I had a serious problem and called my obstetrician. The nurse practitioner said she could hear in my voice that I was depressed. She recommended that I immediately contact a psychologist who specialized in perinatal mood disorders.*

*My first appointment with the psychologist was pleasant. We talked about my symptoms and I felt relieved that someone could understand what I was going through. But when I learned I had something called postpartum depression, I became frightened; I wasn't ready to accept the diagnosis. So after that one session, I decided I was fine and would handle this on my own. When the therapist called a few weeks later to check on how I was doing, I told her I was okay (though I really wasn't), thanked her for her concern and said that I had decided not to continue treatment.*

*The following month I became terribly ill with a case of infectious colitis. I was hospitalized and it took me several weeks to recover. All this time I was trying to care for and breast-feed my infant. As I look back on the events leading up to my hospitalization, I feel that my immune system became compromised when I wasn't taking proper care of myself. Finally, in tears, I called the therapist.*

*I felt like I was in this deep, black hole that I would never be able to climb out of. But I started attending a support group regularly, on top of individual sessions. Though I had resisted taking medication, I finally agreed to try an antidepressant. Gradually my symptoms subsided and I started feeling like myself again. The biggest challenge I faced was learning how to prioritize taking care of myself. But once I started to get enough rest, I had the strength to handle other issues in my life that were contributing to my depression.*

*One of those issues was the lack of support from my husband. After almost a decade of denial, I finally accepted the fact that I was in an unhealthy and verbally abusive marriage. Although a woman's brain chemistry is affected by the hormones during and shortly after pregnancy, environmental factors also can play a role in the situation. In my case, a bad marriage—an unsupportive husband who no longer seemed interested in me and who told me constantly that I was not lovable and everything was my fault—contributed to the onset of my postpartum depression. I felt so unloved and unattractive—who wouldn't be depressed? Although we went on to have another beautiful girl together (during that pregnancy, I worked on ways to prevent depression), the marriage was doomed. I eventually mustered the courage to leave my spouse; we divorced when the children were eight and five years old.*

*As a single mom, I managed to get my figure back and regain my self-confidence. I continue seeing my therapist so I can keep everything in perspective and I continue to take medication as well. I believe that I have emerged a much stronger woman than I was before I had children and with that strength I am able to parent my daughters in a way that will teach them to be aware of and trust in their emotions and self-esteem.*

*Although the journey has been complicated, I've come out on top and achieved my goal: becoming a nurturing, healthy, happy mother as I raise my girls and teach them about life and love. What a wonderful gift this has been! I am eternally grateful to my therapist for the compassion and support she has given me. Her healing work with mothers suffering from postpartum depression is vital for the development of these women as well as their children. I feel very fortunate that I was not only able to recover from this illness but also to flourish. I have come to understand it was definitely an experience of growth and feel strongly that others can recover also.*

---

Following a normal, much desired pregnancy and normal delivery, Ellen's anxiety began as a reaction to her pediatrician's concerns that her newborn baby might have Down syndrome. Waiting two weeks for the results began a vicious cycle of anxiety, depression and sleeplessness that resulted in exhaustion and worsening symptoms. Despite normal test findings, Ellen couldn't stop the worry and obsessive thoughts on her own.

Once she accepted her condition, the healing began and Ellen started to take better care of herself. In therapy, she benefited from cognitive strategies to help her gain control over her fears and her obsessive thoughts. Over time, she explored relationship issues concerning her spouse and her family of origin. Ellen finally admitted, to herself and to me, that her marital relationship was unhealthy, verbally abusive and replayed the relationship of her own parents. As she began to build her coping skills, self-nurture and develop a support network of friends and coworkers, she became stronger, healthier and more autonomous.

# CHAPTER 10

## *Principle III: The Power of Spirituality*

Transformation is the next step in the process of healing from postpartum depression. In finding purpose and gaining wisdom from enduring your experience, you can and will see things more clearly and transform into a better version of yourself. That's not to say the process isn't painful; it's like giving birth. You cannot change without some stretching and pulling. Yet if you have done the necessary work, which hopefully this book and your new understanding of yourself has shown you, you have become altered in a miraculous way.

The point is not just to become different, though, but to become wiser. In the words of spiritual writer Marianne Williamson, "Experience teaches you how to make better choices." Sometimes, she explains in her book *The Age of Miracles*, it's the pain you go through that "transforms you into someone who has the courage to take it on."[1]

As with childbirth, after which your body is modified, you will never look the same as you did before children. But do you want to look the same? Do you want to *stay* the same? If you keep doing what you've always done, you will stagnate. You have to move outside of your comfort zone to grow, to bring new wisdom and understanding to each new situation and event in your life and to make use of all that you have learned. It would be sad if you acquired nothing from such an intense, potentially life-changing ordeal as postpartum depression.

If you cannot identify any ways in which you've changed—if you feel like you haven't really moved on in your life—though your depression may have lifted and you've begun reentering your former activities, then you need to visit a *good* therapist or spiritual teacher to help you find meaning in your illness. I strongly believe it's certainly there, even if you can't perceive it on your own. Sometimes we need help from an objective person to grasp the significance of our feelings and experiences.

As we've discussed in these pages, human beings need to self-reflect and seek to make sense of major life events, such as learning to cope with postpartum depression. In chapter 9, "Principle II: The Power of Hope and Inspiration," we explored how finding significance often seems to be tied to philosophical and religious/spiritual concepts. I believe that, for many, spirituality can help them heal from a postpartum illness and then, afterwards, expand who they are. Before answering *how* this can occur, we must address the *what*.

## THE DIFFERENCE BETWEEN BEING SPIRITUAL AND BEING RELIGIOUS

Spirituality focuses on the inner world of your soul, the region beyond your five physical senses. Spiritual practices are diverse and can incorporate meditation, breathing exercises, chanting, yoga, contemplation or even prayer. But whatever process you choose, the one common and salient feature is that it lets you transcend the physical level and, often, connect with deeper values and meanings, with other people and with the cosmos or the divine realm of life.

Spirituality has been important to mankind for ages, perhaps since the first person looked up at the heavens and wondered what was out there. In the Webcast "Finding Your Spiritual Path," Oprah Winfrey asked three recognized leaders about their definitions of spirituality and how it can help you to find your own path.

I highly recommend you watch the entire video (http://www.oprah.com/spirit/Finding-Your-Spiritual-Path-Oprahs-Best-Life-Series-Webcast-Video). Here are some highlights:

- "It is about our being connected with one another and connected with the cosmos," Reverend Ed Bacon of All Saints Episcopal Church in Pasadena, California, begins in the video. "It is the process of being healed, forgiven, empowered to go into the world, to be fully alive. It's that experience of love that connects you with everyone, connects you with your past, connects you with your future, gives you hope and excitement about going into the next day, going into the next moment."
- Elizabeth Lesser, cofounder of the nonprofit Omega Institute for Holistic Studies, says in the video that spirituality is a part of human nature. Just as we all have the impulse to eat, drink and sleep, spirituality is ingrained in us all and is within everyone's reach. "There's this instinct inside of each and every one of us that there's more to life than meets the eye. Spirituality is our intuition that there is something greater to life than the daily grind. It's the fearlessness to ask the big questions. Who am I? What's my purpose? Where do we go when we die? And how do we live a fully alive, meaningful, giving, generous life when we're here?"
- Michael Bernard Beckwith of Agape International Spiritual Center answers that "love, peace, harmony and wisdom are everlasting qualities. They're real and they're eternal. And so when an individual is connected to those qualities and begins to exude them and express them, at that moment they're in the spirit. And when an individual is mature enough to express that on a regular basis, we can say that they're spiritually mature. Regardless of the temporary problems you may be experiencing, the connection to love, peace and harmony stays with you. That's what carries

you when you're going through tough times. That's what it means to be spiritual."

## SPIRITUALITY VERSUS RELIGION

The terms *spirituality* and *religion* are often confused: Some call the creative source God; others call it universal energy or higher consciousness. But Bacon, Lesser and Beckwith all agree: Spirituality and religion are not necessarily mutually exclusive. You can be one without the other and you can be both at once. Individuals who practice a religion can be spiritual, but they are not always so and many spiritual people do not attend religious services, follow a specific religious practice or even belong to an organized religion.

One definition calls religion an institutionalized system of certain attitudes, beliefs and practices, often including "narratives, symbols, traditions and sacred histories that are intended to give meaning to life or to explain the origin of the universe."[2] According to *Merriam-Webster's Eleventh Collegiate Dictionary*, a religion is "1) the service and worship of God or the supernatural... 2) commitment or devotion to religious faith or observance... 3) a personal set or institutionalized system of religious attitudes, beliefs, and practices... 4) a cause, principle, or system of beliefs held to with ardor and faith."

## ARE YOU SPIRITUAL OR RELIGIOUS?

Many people grapple with this question and are unsure what they believe when it comes to faith. To help you determine where you fit in, here is a survey that I developed. This and other spiritual surveys can be good starting points for you to address aspects of your spirituality and faith. For more questionnaires of this type, visit http://www.beliefnet.com, http://www.spiritualityhealth.com and Oprah.com's "Best of Life: Your Spirituality" workbook pages at http://www.oprah.com/spirit/Oprahs-Best-Life-Series-Spirituality-Workbooks.

### Spiritual Survey

1. Do you believe in something beyond the physical, material world of the five senses? Where does that spiritual world reside—outside of yourself, within yourself, in all of us? Do you think there is a connection among all people?
2. Do you practice a specific organized religion? If so, which one? Do you attend services or follow certain customs or rituals? Why or why not?
3. If you don't belong to a specific organized religion, do you still consider yourself to be spiritual? Is there any other group you are affiliated with (for example, a meditation group, Kabbalah group, Qigong healing group or prayer circle)?
4. Do you believe in an afterlife? Heaven? Reincarnation?
5. How often do you practice your spirituality? Daily, weekly or yearly? Do you attend any spiritual events or celebrations? Which ones?
6. How does your spirituality help you in your daily life? Is this something you turn to in difficult times, when things are going well or both?
7. Are your friends and/or partners spiritual or religious, too? How important is it to you that they are on the same spiritual path or of the same religion?
8. How does your spirituality enhance your life and your relationships?

## SPIRITUALITY IN MY CLIENTS

Early in my clients' treatment, I discuss this subject frankly by asking what religious or spiritual practices they engage in, how frequently they observe these practices and in what situations they turn to them for comfort or support. Some women are surprised by my questions and to others they seem odd. People tend to see a dichotomy between a medical healer and a spiritual one. Yet where they may see a contradiction, I see these as interrelated and complementary. I encourage clients to use their religious and/or spiritual practices not only as a way of coping with postpartum illness and symptoms but also to explore and be open-minded to other beliefs that also could offer value.

To be sure that I don't influence someone, which would be inappropriate, I avoid bringing up my own religious beliefs or spiritual path unless a client asks me about it directly. As a health practitioner, I may guide and facilitate clients' explorations of religious and/or spiritual paths that they feel might suit them, but I'm always cautious to respect clients' beliefs and not to sway them in any direction. They need to decide on their own whether they want to rely on such traditional religious observances as attending services and praying in a church, synagogue or mosque or seeking guidance from their religious leaders, such as a pastor, priest, rabbi or imam. They might want to join support groups sponsored by their chosen houses of worship or affiliated with their religions—or even groups that are connected with different religious organizations. Some clients are drawn to non-Western spiritual paths, such as meditation, yoga, mindfulness courses or chanting. They may attend 12-step programs or spiritual retreats, listen to stirring speakers or read inspirational books. Any ritual, belief or practice that provides comfort and helps your self-healing and self-reflection can aid you in recovery from your postpartum disorder and transformation.

## SPIRITUALITY IN MEDICAL AND PSYCHOLOGICAL HEALING

Does the discussion of faith or spirituality have a place in psychotherapy? Is it appropriate to be talking to clients about religion, mysticism and soul-related topics while practicing psychology, a discipline defined as a *science* of mind and behavior?

The Canadian Counseling and Psychotherapy Association (CCPA), a national organization dedicated to enhancing the profession of counseling in Canada, has explored the role of faith in psychotherapy. In an online commentary titled "Benefits of Faith," CCPA posed the question: what advantage does faith have in a therapeutic environment? The CCPA states: "Faith is capable of providing a foundation of support, a source of hope and comfort, and a place of solitude and refuge during troubling times." The article concludes, "Integrating faith and psychology is not a difficult task, rather it is sort of a natural evolution. It is faith that has the ability of employing unconditional trust, therefore allowing our minds to completely relax and reach a higher plateau of peace."[3]

Another confirmation of faith's positive effect on mental health comes from the American Psychological Association (APA). The results of a self-reported study of religious faith and spirituality among 236 people recovering from addictions were presented at the APA's annual conference. The findings, detailed in the presentation "Religious Denomination Affiliation and Psychological Health: Results From a Substance Abuse Population," indicate that "higher levels of religious faith and spirituality were associated with several positive mental health outcomes, including more optimism about life and higher resilience to stress, which may help contribute to the recovery process." The researchers stated that the findings were "similar to previous studies that show people recovering from substance abuse tend to place great importance on prayer, belief in a God and a strong sense of faith."[4]

The book *Mind/Body Health: The Effects of Attitudes, Emotions and Relationships*, cowritten by Keith Karren, Lee Smith, Brent Hafen and Kathryn J. Frandsen, devotes several chapters to the healing power of faith and hope and to the effect this has on physical and mental well-being. The authors discuss the work of several renowned scientists and physicians who have attributed importance to faith in healing. One example is the scientist Deirdre Davis Bingham, who stated, "It is in the nature of scientific inquiry (and human consciousness) that major advances come from people who look at things in a different way—who break through the shell of their immediate nesting egg" (referring to matryoshka dolls, the famous Russian painted doll "eggs" that nest inside one another). Davis appears to be one scientist who investigates by looking for answers beyond the concrete world and what we already know.

"That is not to say that faith should replace modern medicine," Karren and his coauthors write. "Instead, it should be used in conjunction with modern medicine—used to enhance the effects of medicine and to strengthen its impact. Even staunch medical practitioners recognize that faith plays a vital part in the healing process." They cite the sixteenth century surgeon Ambrose Pare, who noted in a surgical report, "I dressed the wound, and God healed it."[5]

Physicians like cardiologist Herbert Benson make a case for the power of our minds over healing our bodies. In his groundbreaking book *Beyond the Relaxation Response*, he introduces an idea he calls the "faith factor," explaining that "our personal powers and potential for well-being are shaped by the negative or positive ways we think." He continues, "Medical and scientific research is demonstrating ever more clearly that the things we can touch, taste, and measure may frequently have to take a backseat to what we *perceive* or *believe* to be real." If the mind is that strong, he says, then its beliefs and faith can play a key role in generating a response in the body. He adds, "It's how we interpret reality, or how our body 'sees' the concrete world around us, that is important." Benson points to countless studies that have shown this to be true in relieving a myriad of disorders: headaches, angina pains, hypertension, insomnia, hyperventilation attacks, backaches, panic attacks, high cholesterol levels, overall stress and the symptoms of anxiety, like nausea, vomiting, diarrhea, constipation, short temper and the inability to get along with others. Even cancer can be mitigated, according to this doctor.[6]

Researcher and author Joan Borysenko, PhD, partnered with Benson and another medical doctor, Ilan Kutz, to found the Mind-Body Clinic at Beth Israel Hospital in Boston (now part of Beth Israel/Deaconess Medical Center). As director of the clinic, Borysenko studied cancer patients who were considered long-term survivors and she found that the one trait they had in common was a strong sense of faith. In her landmark book *Minding the Body,*

*Mending the Mind*, she discusses the science of healing and the effect the mind has on illness as well as how the mind can be used to heal the body.

We need to start realizing that healing and faith are not contradictory or dichotomous concepts. We have been used to thinking that physical healing belongs solely in the realm of medicine and that faith belongs squarely in the religious community. Anyone who so much as suggested that healing was a common sphere of influence was ostracized. And on the other side of the equation, we regarded ideas like faith healing as the property of crackpots, charlatans and scoundrels. They brought to mind either religious fanatics or traveling snake oil salesmen who dispensed—for a price—tonics and potions to desperate but naïve followers, often in rural, medically underserved areas. Today there's a growing movement within the medical community and among mental health providers to address the common ground between these subjects respectfully. Professionals in the medical field are beginning to accept the fact that faith is a useful tool in healing and the general public is coming to the same conclusion.

At the same time that we're witnessing changes in conventional medicine, we're also seeing integrative or holistic medicine beginning to gain credence. Among practitioners of traditional medicine in hospitals, universities and medical schools in many parts of the world, there is a growing willingness to explore alternative, nonconventional methods. Thousands of well-known and well-respected medical facilities and physicians are now at least willing to consider integrative methods in treating patients; some doctors, such as Andrew Weil and Deepak Chopra, are drawing heavily on these techniques.

In a joint effort by Case Western Reserve University, George Washington University School of Medicine and Duke University Medical Center, researchers found that "clinical studies are beginning to clarify how spirituality and religion can contribute to the coping strategies of many patients with severe, chronic, and terminal conditions." At one time, it would have been unheard of for such eminent medical establishments to participate in research on this subject. In its review of numerous prior studies, the team explored the advisability of doctors' discussing spiritual issues with their clients, the professional boundaries between physicians and the hospital chaplain and "medical ethics at a time when researchers are beginning to appreciate the spiritual aspects of coping with illness," as the article "Physicians and Patient Spirituality: Professional Boundaries, Competency, and Ethics" in the *Annals of Internal Medicine* put it.[7]

"Both doctors and patients alike are bonding with the philosophy of integrative medicine and its whole-person approach," WebMD writes, "designed to treat the person, not just the disease. IM, as it's often called, depends on a partnership between the patient and the doctor, where the goal is to treat the mind, body, and spirit, all at the same time." This speaks to the shifting tides in medicine, which these days grant a greater respect for spirituality practices. One example of this type of care can be found at the Duke Center for Integrative Medicine, which, according to WebMD, "combines conventional Western medicine with alternative or complementary treatments, such as herbal medicine, acupuncture, massage, biofeedback, yoga, and stress reduction techniques—all in the effort to treat the whole person."[8] Additionally, UCLA has opened an East-West medical center, where doctors make presentations with titles like "The Healing Approach of Eastern Medicine; An Integrative East-West Medicine Approach to the Treatment of Pain" and "Optimizing Health and Achieving Wellness Through Integrative East-West Medicine."

## CAN SPIRITUALITY AND FAITH HELP HEALING?

This seems to be a topic much debated, both publicly and scientifically, and that polarizes laypeople and medical practitioners alike. While numerous books and press articles claim that spirituality has been found to promote healing, a seemingly equal number take the opposite view. And some people in the medical community assert that a person cannot isolate all of the variables necessary to prove or disprove unequivocally the effect of spirituality on healing. A

Web site devoted to online courses for surgical technicians (http://onlinesurgicaltechniciancourses.com) recently reviewed twenty-five intriguing scientific studies about faith, prayer and healing. Its conclusion: "Some studies seem to show that faith and prayer can have a positive effect on healing, while others seem to show that there is no benefit at all to these types of intercessions."[9] Doctors and others in the medical community have continued to explore the subject for decades.

In searching the Cochrane Library, a collection of databases in medicine and other healthcare specialties, I found many articles about the application of various spiritual methods, like yoga, prayer and acupuncture, to a variety of health-related problems, from breast cancer and HIV/AIDS to substance abuse and weight loss. But there was no easy answer to the query, no universal agreement on whether faith, through spirituality and/or religious practice, can aid health and healing. For example, though a Johns Hopkins study of one hundred chronically ill adults found a small improvement in reported energy when the subjects were encouraged to use spiritual coping mechanisms, there was no significant improvement in their pain, mood, perception of health, illness intrusiveness or self-efficacy. And a Cochrane review of intercessory prayer found conflicting evidence of a positive effect but still concluded that it "was interesting enough to justify further study."[10]

When I explored more general impressions about the correlation between health and faith, I found a varied collection of articles. Let's discuss a few that are informative.

An article in *The American Journal of Psychiatry* titled "The Healing Power of Faith: Science Explores Medicine's Last Great Frontier" discusses the work of Harold Koenig, MD, a family practitioner turned psychiatrist who observed that "patients who were active in their religions not only lived healthier and happier lives" but also experienced "miracles of health" that did not occur in nonreligious patients. As he began to study the data, Koenig discovered "abundant but often overlooked evidence that people who are in tune with their religions have healthier lifestyles and fewer mental and physical disorders." This actually led him to change careers; he became director of the Duke University Center for the Study of Religion/Spirituality and Health. In his investigation, Koenig found that there were two ways in which religious faith had preventive and health-enhancing effects. First, "religious people with a strong social support network often have their diseases diagnosed earlier, become actively involved in their treatments, and follow their caregivers' instructions more closely than do less religious people." Second, people who are more religious tend to avoid unhealthy habits such as smoking and drinking alcohol.[11]

Many benefits for health and well-being can accrue from spiritual and religious beliefs, rituals and practices, writes Ellen Idler, PhD, of Yale in an article printed in the newsletter *Spirituality in Higher Education.* "These experiences lift us up out of our narrow selves," she states, "and give us a glimpse—if only temporary—of another way to view things as a part, however small, of a larger picture." She indicates that rites of passage, such as coming-of-age rituals, can be particularly helpful for adolescents and young adults in providing rules for living. Idler cites research from the University of Michigan that found high school seniors who had religious involvement had healthier lifestyle and behavioral habits, including lower rates of alcohol use, cigarette smoking, marijuana use, fighting and carrying weapons and higher rates of wearing seatbelts and eating healthy food. (The study analzyed data from 135 schools in forty-eight states.) As people mature into adulthood, she points out, religious communities provide social supports that reduce stress, have a positive influence on health and lower mortality. In addition, besides contributing to healthier, happier lives, "spiritual and religious practices have their own *intrinsic value* and are sufficient as ends unto themselves," Idler concludes.[12]

In an article called "Spirituality and Health: Is There a Relationship?" (published in the *Journal of Health Psychology*) author Carl E. Thoresen of Stanford University states, "The role of spiritual and religious factors in health, viewed from a scientific perspective, has been yielding interesting if not intriguing results. In general, studies have reported fairly consistent positive relationships with physical health, mental health, and substance abuse outcomes."[13]

A study on faith healing, published by the *Southern Medical Journal*, reports surprising improvements in vision and hearing after using proximal intercessory prayer for healing, suggesting that praying for another person's health may be medically beneficial if the two people are in close proximity.[14]

A group of researchers at UCLA explored facets of spirituality as predictors of adjustment to cancer. As the subtitle of their article in the *Journal of Consulting and Clinical Psychology* put it, they were looking to uncover the relative contributions of having faith and finding meaning. "Spirituality is a multidimensional construct," the authors state, "and little is known about how its distinct dimensions jointly affect well-being." They conducted a pair of studies that examined two components of spiritual well-being (meaning/peace and faith) and their interaction, first in 418 breast cancer patients (Study 1) and then in 165 cancer survivors (Study 2). In Study 1, subjects who had higher baseline scores and an increase in meaning/peace over six months were expected to experience a reduction in depression and an increase in energy over twelve months, while "Study 2 revealed that an increase in meaning/peace was related to improved mental health and lower cancer-related distress."

The authors write that an increase in faith was related to increased cancer-related growth. (I'm assuming that the participants increased their faith because they had increased cancer growth and not the other way around.) But both studies found "significant interactions between meaning/peace and faith in predicting adjustment." The authors conclude, "the ability to find meaning and peace in life is the more influential contributor to favorable adjustment during cancer survivorship."[15] (It is important to note here that this study looked specifically at *emotional adjustment* to disease, not medical healing.)

Despite all the evidence, however, and the growing open-mindedness that the American Medical Association is beginning to adopt regarding the integration of Eastern and Western medical traditions, it is still up to you to decide how spiritual or religious practices can affect your own healing process.

The connection between faith and healing has attracted not only the medical community but the American public as well. This is evident in the explosion of magazine articles and TV shows on the subject as well as Internet programs such as *A Balanced Life,* which features guests like Deepak Chopra, MD, discussing the Hindu principle of dharma, giving back, finding your life's purpose and more. Perhaps because of the world's troubled economy or a shift in consciousness, there seems to be a trend these days to look for happiness in some way other than through material possessions.

When I placed a recent issue of *O, the Oprah Magazine* on the coffee table in my waiting room, I glanced at the back page and saw a picture of Oprah practicing Transcendental Meditation (TM) alongside other meditators in Fairfield, Iowa. As a long-time meditator myself, I felt an immediate kinship to her and read the article to see her opinions. It occurred to me that since Oprah is such a trendsetter, when spirituality becomes a hot topic for her, it's a sign of a positive shift in our national or perhaps world consciousness. In the article, Oprah explains that she went to Fairfield (known affectionately as TM Town) to film an episode of *Next Chapter,* an interview program for the Oprah Winfrey Network that's shot on location. She describes her experience of TM as "powerfully energizing yet calming" and was so taken by the practice that she arranged to have TM teachers instruct everyone in her company who wanted to learn. Oprah and her staff have starting meditating every day. The results: reports of better sleep, reduced migraines, improved relationships and greater productivity and creativity.

In the same issue of *O,* Oprah reveals her "positive intention" for the year. Consistent with her upbeat attitude, she says she is going to approach the year as one of promise and the beginning of a spiritual revolution.[16]

Oprah also produces two Webcast series, *Soul* (http://www.oprah.com/oprahradio/About-Oprahs-Soul-Series-Webcast) and *Best Life* (http://www.oprah.com/oprahshow/Watch-the-Best-Life-Series-Webcasts), plus a *Spirit Channel* podcast (http://www.oprah.com/podcasts/anewearth.xml).

## NONTRADITIONAL SPIRITUALITY

If you haven't decided yet whether spirituality can benefit your physical and mental health, consider that spirituality doesn't necessarily mean praying, chanting or meditating (although it can). It often appears in the most surprising places when you are open and willing to look for it.

A perfect example can be found in an interview with designer Gabrielle Blair on writer Gretchen Rubin's blog The Happiness Project. *Time* magazine named Design Mom, Blair's blog, a top Web site and found Blair's viewpoint to be refreshingly positive, even inspirational. Many of the things Blair discusses in her interview with Rubin are similar to the coping strategies I list in chapter 8, "Principle I: Finding Ways to Heal": get enough sleep, feel gratitude, enjoy the small pleasures of life, include sex and love in your life, nurture your interests and be actively creative. Blair states, "The happiest, most content people I know in my own life are actively creative in some way, shape, or form. Creativity looks different on each of us…if we're expressing our talents and nurturing our interests…happiness is happening."[17]

When asked about the concept of happiness, Blair reveals, "I've realized how much of me feeling happy is a choice. I'm still just figuring it out, but I try my best to make that choice every hour of every day. When I'm feeling negative emotions, I take responsibility for them and acknowledge that I can actively choose to feel happier that very minute. That very minute! How empowering is that?"

I highly recommend you read the entire interview (http://happiness-project.com/happiness_project/2012/02/id-admired-gabrielle-blairs-blog-design-momat-the-intersection-of-design-and-motherhoodfor-a-long-time-clearly-im/). Blair is a great role model, such a happy person with a zest for life. I suggest we all adopt her attitude.

## SEARCHING FOR SPIRITUALITY

As you search for inspiration, think about this question: What spiritual practices help you connect to higher consciousness or God? I thought the best way to find out what helps people was to ask them. So I took an informal survey, posting this question on my blog and querying people in my daily life.

The responses represent a broad collection of spiritual and New Age practices as well as established religious rituals and behaviors; all are legitimate. Here are some responses I gathered:

- Prayer, 12-step meetings, breathing and walking.
- Running and dancing.
- I'm Catholic and I dearly love saying my rosary. I can say it anywhere and always carry several with me. I also enjoy lighting candles at church for guidance with health and other issues or for those in need of some extra help.
- I find prayer helps me let go and connect to a more positive power.
- Greeting each person every day with a smile.
- Exercising my sense of humor—find something funny every day and have a good laugh!
- I start each day trying to be better than I was yesterday.
- Saying the Tehillim for the people I love helps me a lot. Praying directly and asking God for help where I'm limited to help myself helps me to feel I'm not as alone with my problems.
- Reiki.
- Sometimes I call my 12-step sponsor or go to a meeting. Sometimes I write and in that creative space I develop "flow," which I consider to be a spiritual place of refreshment and renewal.
- Walking in the forest or by a body of water, swimming, dancing, listening to a dharma, calling a friend for laughter, doing yoga, biking.
- Volunteering is something that draws you out of your misery and "giving" always makes you feel better too.
- When I wake up, I spend the first thirty minutes reading the Zohar (the Kabbalistic text) to start my day off in a positive way, before going to work. As time permits, I use

various spiritual tools, meditate and read spiritual books and listen to CDs or watch DVDs that are inspiring.

Feel free to borrow some of these ideas if you want to try something new or just expand your own repertoire. And then, pay it forward! After all, it's about sharing and connecting; let's reach out and assist one another on our journeys of transformation.

Although I do not lead clients in their spiritual search, I recommend books, CDs and DVDs and often lend works by my favorite inspirational authors. A compilation of titles that I find inspiring can be found in appendix A. They span a variety of spiritual healing perspectives. My hope is that you'll find at least a couple that resonate with you. If you know of or discover a book, CD or DVD that you think is a must-see or must-read, let me know and I'll pass it along via my blog.

There are many places to find wonderful spiritual films, magazines, books, conferences, workshops and resources. This list of organizations and sources is meant to be only a beginning, not a comprehensive guide. Again, if you know of a great source, tell me and I'll add it. In order to know what is best for you personally, you'll have to check these out and make that decision for yourself.

- The Spiritual Cinema Circle (http://spiritualcinemacircle.com) is a DVD club that features transformational films. Each month, members receive four inspiring videos—movies you probably would not see in your local theatre. You can try it out for free. Another option is to stream videos through GaiamTV (http://gaiamtv.com), a sister company to the Spiritual Cinema Circle. Why not form a monthly film group with friends, which could provide an entertaining evening of viewing followed by discussion?
- Kabbalah University offers a free three-day trial membership (http://ukabbalah.com or 888-898-8358). Here you can learn online about the Kabbalah (an ancient mystical tradition) and how to apply its teachings in

your daily life. This nonprofit site offers thousands of video lessons and practical tools, plus a supportive global community to help you study, grow and transform. Buttons link you to various courses, like Parenting with Consciousness. You can also connect to a personal Kabbalah teacher for one-on-one instruction.

- Each month Eckhart Tolle TV (http://eckharttolletv.com) presents Tolle giving a talk, leading a live online meditation and conducting a Q&A via a Webcast in which you can participate. Additional teachings and guided practices by Kim Eng are also offered, plus seminars, global gatherings and other events for spiritual awakening.
- The Transcendental Meditation Program (http://www.tm.org or 888-LEARN TM/888-532-7686) offers the opportunity to study with a personal teacher. Transcendental Meditation, a simple, natural, effortless process, is practiced for twenty minutes twice daily. It relieves stress and brings inner peace, enhanced health and well-being and possibly enlightenment.
- Author and spiritual teacher Susan Shumsky sells books, audio and seminars for intuitional and spiritual development. According to her Web site (http://www.divinerevelation.org), she has practiced self-development and spirituality for more than forty years.
- Oprah Winfrey's Web site offers amazing podcasts, online interviews and other resources with some of the top spiritual teachers. At Oprah's Spirit Channel (http://www.oprah.com/podcasts/anewearth.xml), Oprah and leading spiritual thinkers, teachers and authors talk about matters of the soul, spirit and self. On the spirit page of Oprah's Web site (http://www.oprah.com/spirit.html), get to know yourself, transform your life and find inspiration in the human spirit. Oprah's *Soul Series* Webcast (http://www.oprah.com/oprahradio/About-Oprahs-Soul-Series-Webcast) has uplifting interviews with spiritual teachers like Jon Kabat-Zinn and Eckhart Tolle.

- Shambhala Publications (888-424-2329 or at http://www.shambhala.com) offers resources to learn about Shambhala. You can join this Buddhist meditation community or just enjoy its many books and tapes that promote health and well-being.
- The Omega Institute for Holistic Studies (http://eomega.org) holds trainings and seminars in wellness and personal growth. It also offers an opportunity to connect to gifted teachers like Elizabeth Lesser, Byron Katie, Debbie Ford and James Van Praagh.
- In keeping with its tagline "Changing the consciousness of the planet one event at a time," Mishka Productions (http://mishkaproductions.com) holds weekend events and Celebrate Your Life conferences (http://mishkaproductions.com/content/celebrate-your-life) that feature well-known spiritual speakers.
- HayHouse Radio (http://www.hayhouseradio.com) streams live programs by Louise Hay and others. It features weekly shows with authors and special live online events.

Recently, the concept of the "faith factor" was used as the basis for a fictional book titled *Nexus: A Neo Novel* by Deborah Morrison and Arvind Singh and their blog (http://nexusnovel.wordpress.com/blog-posts). As their Web site describes it, the book "follows the soul-searching journey of an odd mix of people thrown together at a spiritual retreat designed to help them cope with personal pain and find the centre of their being." In this story, those who have the faith factor experience fewer health problems, less stress and greater inner peace.

I also recommend a short but powerful book called *Who Moved My Cheese?* by Spencer Johnson. This *New York Times* bestseller, a simple parable about four characters who deal with unexpected change as they look for the "cheese" they previously took for granted, promotes the idea of being open to change and will encourage you on your journey of transformation. This short story is one you can identify with as you ask yourself about your own perception of change and how *you* deal with it, too.

*Who Moved My Cheese?* can be a good tool for examining your own fear of change and resistance to going in a new direction—to try something new, look at something in a novel way or consider a new possibility. I recommend this book to help you assess your own ability to let go of outdated fears, to change and to enjoy the adventure of finding a new, improved you.

---

### IN HER OWN WORDS: ANNA'S STORY

*I glance briefly at my two young children playing nearby and a wave of joy and peace runs through me that's so overwhelming my eyes well up. They have changed me in ways they most likely will never understand. It wasn't long ago that I was wandering the painful depths of postpartum anxiety and depression. Looking back now, I almost can't believe what I went through...was it just a really bad dream? As someone who had previously never been depressed, I had no idea what was wrong with me.*

*For months I was in a haze of anxiety and sadness. I doubted that I'd ever be my old self again and, at the time, being me—being normal—was all I wanted. There were days when I felt paralyzed, almost unable to function, when just taking a shower seemed overwhelming. At my lowest point, I was scared that I was going to get into my car, start driving and never stop...just run away. My path to recovery began the morning I first sat on my therapist's couch. I sat there sobbing, feeling lost, scared, alone, discouraged—it was a moment I will never forget. Little did I know that my journey out of postpartum darkness would change me forever.*

*Maybe there was a reason for my suffering, a lesson to be learned. Maybe this was the plan of someone or something much greater than myself. Before my experience with postpartum depression, I'm not sure I was ever really present in my own life. It was a life overflowing with blessings, but I was missing it all by letting it pass me by! My mind was always running busily like an Internet search engine, making list after list of all the things I needed to get done that day, going from one task to the next. While I was doing one thing, my mind was already two steps ahead. I felt accomplished and that's how I lived. When you feel good and life seems to be going well, you don't know any different way to live, so it's easy to get caught up in the day-to-day madness and take for granted the little things that really matter.*

*But as I emerged from my postpartum fog, I began to change. Things that had been important to me before weren't so critical anymore. As I started feeling better, the appreciation I had for just feeling normal again was life altering. I also realized that I had "tasked" away the first two years of my oldest child's life, so much so that I couldn't remember a time when I just sat and enjoyed her. I had taken for granted all the gifts I had been given, the simple things in life: health, friendship, beautiful children, a loving husband. Where was my appreciation for all of these things? It wasn't until deep suffering was bestowed upon me that I was truly able to appreciate them.*

*I am better now than ever before. The lessons I've learned from my battle with postpartum depression are invaluable and when I say that I have been changed forever, I mean it in the best way possible. I feel blessed that I was given the opportunity to reevaluate my life in time to change it. I know that I am a work in progress and always will be. But my eyes are open to real pain and suffering and because of that I wake up every day thankful—for my blessings and for just feeling like myself again, something I took for granted most of my life.*

*When I think of the prevalence of postpartum depression and the number of mothers around us who are trying to find their ways out, it is heartbreaking. If you are reading this in the midst of such suffering, please hang on, stay strong and have faith. You absolutely will be yourself again...and you may actually emerge better than ever.*

---

Anna was a woman who was successful and so busy that she never experienced the joy of the present moment. She was always active—moving from one thing to the next, looking ahead rather than focusing on the current activity. She was a compulsive over-achiever and enjoyed her own success: a woman who knew how to get things done, but seldom enjoyed the process.

In treatment, in addition to working on symptom remission, we concentrated on ways to strike a balance in her life among work, family and leisure. She learned to refocus on mindfulness and be present-oriented, rather than goal-focused. We also worked on anxiety reduction and being more centered through relaxation, self-awareness and breathing techniques. Anna tended to neglect herself in order to get more tasks checked off her to-do list; she needed encouragement to prioritize self-care. She rarely stopped to reflect on her own satisfaction, a sense of gratitude or the simple pleasures of life. It was life-altering for this driven woman to shift her attention and begin to value her relationships, devoting time to her family and enjoying playtime with her children.

# CHAPTER 11

## *Faith to Get You Through Life's Challenges*

I have explained how faith and spirituality can aid you and have a positive effect on your physical and mental health. In troubled times, everyone can use some faith to help them cope and weather the storm. Next is a client's account of such a situation.

---

### MARIA'S STORY

*Maria, one of my youngest clients, was in her mid-twenties, yet mature beyond her years. She was referred to me by her boss and one of her friends at work. Both were concerned because she seemed more emotional than usual and not as happy. At the time I met this attractive, charming woman, she was in a good marriage, had a three-year-old daughter and was pregnant with her second child. Nonetheless, Maria was insecure. Her coworkers were right to be concerned: She had suffered depression before and although she was excited about this planned pregnancy, she was already withdrawing socially, losing weight and crying a lot.*

*Her intake appointment confirmed my suspicion that she was experiencing antepartum depression—a combination of symptoms of anxiety and panic attacks, including palpitations, difficulty catching her breath, sweating, nausea, lightheadedness and the feeling that she was losing control. In addition, she was losing her sense of joy and feeling sad, which are classic features of clinical depression. During that first session, I learned that Maria had been having these symptoms for the past month, but perhaps more important, this wasn't her first encounter with depression. She had been in therapy for the condition at various other periods in her life.*

*Her first episode of depression occurred at age fifteen after she broke up with a boyfriend. At that time, a combination of medication and individual psychotherapy proved useful. Following that period, Maria seemed to do well, although she reported mood fluctuations and sometimes significant anxiety, often coinciding with her monthly menstrual period. This is a sign of hormonal sensitivity and one of several risk factors for antepartum and postpartum mood disorders. (Other risk factors are discussed in chapter 2, "The Postpartum Continuum.") Maria told me her teenage years were rather "stormy," with her parents even encouraging her to seek professional therapy to find better ways of coping with her monthly bouts of anger and irritability.*

*In her junior year of high school, Maria met George and they became sweethearts. She fell deeply in love. They dated exclusively during school and married several years after graduation. Maria told me that she attended a few years of junior college, pursuing a degree in early childhood education while she worked at a local daycare center.*

*Because she and George loved children, they decided not to wait to start a family, even though they were only in their early twenties. Soon Maria got pregnant and, shortly after the birth of her daughter, she dropped out of college to focus on her job and baby girl. Maria had some attention and organizational problems, so school had always been a challenge, which resulted in low self-esteem and doubts that she could succeed in college. Besides, Maria told me, she really enjoyed being with her baby and dreamed of quitting work to become a full-time stay-at-home mom.*

*Although she experienced some mild to moderate postpartum depression in the first few months, a brief course of therapy seemed to help and she was feeling better in a short time. However, women who have postpartum depression once are at higher risk for recurrence and sometimes the symptoms start earlier the next time, even during pregnancy. Thus, it was not surprising that a few years later, when Maria became pregnant again, she began having symptoms of panic and anxiety so severe that she wound up in the hospital at the end of her first trimester. After being released a few days later, she was referred to an outpatient psychiatrist who unfortunately was inexperienced in treating antepartum depression. He told Maria that for the safety of her unborn baby she could not take any medication during pregnancy. This left her feeling hopeless and desperate, she told me, since her symptoms were becoming worse and she still had more than six months left before delivery.*

*As a clinical psychologist, I cannot advise clients about a medication's potential risk to the fetus, but I do highly recommend that they seek the advice and services of a psychiatrist knowledgeable in perinatal issues. This is particularly important with pregnant and breast-feeding moms, as the safety of mother and baby needs to be evaluated and monitored closely. In the state where I practice, as in most states, psychologists cannot prescribe drugs; this is the domain of psychiatry. However, what I can tell a client is that there is always a risk-benefit ratio; the risks need to be weighed against the benefits of a non-depressed woman who is eating and sleeping well, which also has an impact on the health of the fetus. There is no one-size-fits-all solution in this type of situation; each woman needs to be evaluated individually to determine what is in the best interest of both her and her baby.*

*In order to empower clients to make their own decisions, I often provide them with Web addresses and phone numbers of two nonprofit organizations, MotherRisk (http://www.motherrisk.org) and the Organization of Teratology Information Specialists (http://www.otispregnancy.org), which provide evidence-based, clinical information to clients and healthcare professionals about exposure to prescription and over-the-counter medications as well as possible effects of particular drugs on pregnancy and breast-feeding. There is nothing wrong with doing some of your own homework and being prepared to discuss with your psychiatrist what you have learned and to ask any questions you may have during your appointment. If your doctor is uncomfortable with your being an informed partner and participant in your own health plan, you should probably look for another physician, one who can accept you as a team member. After all, the health and safety of you and your baby depend on it!*

*I referred Maria to a local psychiatrist who was well-informed about medication that's considered relatively safe for pregnancy and we began working together on a weekly basis to get her symptoms under control. She started to improve within a few weeks, although I continued to treat her on a less frequent basis as the months went by. When her delivery date came near, we set up a postpartum plan to prepare for the hormonal cascade that was coming as well as other stressors, such as lack of sleep and the added responsibility of caring for a second child. Maria had a strong marriage, a sound family support system and a group of good friends, all assets she could count on if she became symptomatic again.*

*Following her baby's delivery, Maria did have some symptoms of postpartum depression and anxiety. So in keeping with her psychiatrist's recommendation, she increased her medication and the frequency of our therapy sessions. Because she was worried about the effect of her medication on the baby, she decided to stop nursing. (Even when a prescribing doctor thinks it's safe to continue breast-feeding, some women choose to cease breast-feeding to avoid any potential risk). The baby seemed to thrive and over the next few weeks she gained weight and slept longer, as she appeared to be a healthy, flourishing child.*

*All of which made the events that followed so unexpected and dreadful that I shiver to recall them.*

*I am always a bit alarmed when my cell phone rings in the early hours of the morning, before I go to work, as my friends and family rarely call then. I make it a point to answer these unexpected, infrequent calls, as it's often a client having an emergency. This time the call was from Maria's sister, who was sobbing so hysterically that I could barely understand her as she told me Maria's baby had died during the night. Sudden infant death syndrome (SIDS) was the likely cause. She asked me to call Maria, thinking I might help her through this tragedy somehow; the family didn't know what else to do. They knew Maria trusted me and we had a good therapeutic relationship.*

*After hanging up, I felt numb, frozen, shocked. I have been in practice a long time and, unfortunately, have heard many tragic stories, yet I still react emotionally when something horrible happens to a friend, relative or one of my clients. I dreaded making the call to Maria. What could I say to someone who just lost her two-month-old child? How could I console her? I shuddered when I thought about how terrifying the fear of SIDS is to all parents.*

*According to many sources, including the nonprofit American SIDS Institute (http://www.sids.org), almost all SIDS deaths occur without any warning or symptoms, when the infant is thought to be sleeping. The American SIDS Institute reports that in a typical situation, "parents check on their supposedly sleeping infant to find him or her dead. This is the worst tragedy parents can face, a tragedy which leaves them with a sadness and a feeling of vulnerability that lasts throughout their lives. Since medicine cannot tell them why their baby died, they blame themselves and often other innocent people. Their lives and those around them are changed forever."*[1]

*I placed the call. Maria was hysterical and told me between sobs that she had woken up in the morning to find her baby dead. She requested that I attend the funeral service at her church, saying she really needed me to be there. I am usually careful about maintaining boundaries with clients but decided this was an exception and so I went to her church for the funeral. We stayed closely in touch for the next few weeks, sometimes by phone and sometimes with her coming in for sessions. In addition to the grieving, her mood plummeted. Frequently I assessed her suicidality, but despite her intense pain, her religious belief kept this from being an option. I encouraged her to see her psychiatrist more often and to consider increasing the dosage of her antidepressant. But she did not want to do this, perhaps because she realized that no amount of medication could bring her baby back. In therapy I used many coping strategies, interventions and other techniques with her. However, mostly I just sat with her and let her cry and grieve over this devastating loss, knowing that only time and her faith would pull her through.*

*Throughout the months that followed, Maria held tightly to her faith and belief in God, using prayer and the outpouring of love and support she received from her church and fellow parishioners to help her to mourn and eventually begin to heal. I'd like to believe I helped in some small way, as certainly the loving support of her family did. But truly I think it was her religious belief and observance, her connection to her church and some divine presence through her faith that gave her the stamina to continue to live day-by-day with the suffering she had to endure.*

*All that happened more than five years ago. Maria has had another baby girl and she now volunteers as a room mother in her older daughter's grade school. Recently she decided to return to college to study pediatric nursing. I still see her occasionally for treatment and we both are brought to tears whenever we revisit the loss and pain of that period. Overall, Maria has transformed into a strong-willed, mature woman grounded in her faith and determined that her belief in God and the support of her church will help her overcome any future challenge. I have no doubt that is true.*

---

## FAITH AND HEALING

Whether it's expressed through established religious observance or unconventional practices, faith in the divine aspect of existence can provide a healing value. The boundaries between the established medical community and religious and spiritual healing communities are becoming more porous than ever.

In *The River of Light: Jewish Mystical Awareness*, ordained rabbi, scholar and spiritual leader Lawrence Kushner writes, "Possessed of almost poetic promise, [consciousness] is also the legitimate object of scientific inquiry. It brings together many of the strands of psychotherapy, from Freud to transpersonal psychology. It appears on the outer edges of theoretical physics and biochemistry. It is at home both in theology and mythology. Perhaps, we imagine, it is the location of a long-awaited synthesis of some of the great truth traditions of humanity." He further discusses the concept of light as a metaphor for consciousness. According to Kushner, "Recent work in astrophysics and cosmology tells of a creation event that is astonishingly parallel to the one described by spiritual tradition. Perhaps light is, in some sense, consciousness pulsing within and unifying all being."[2]

You may be asking yourself: What does spirituality have to do with healing from postpartum depression and how does that relate to transforming my life and myself? You need to reflect on this yourself, but I will give you my thoughts about the relationship between these ideas and how this can help you on your journey of healing and transformation.

Spirituality, to me, is the interconnectedness of everyone with the Divine Creator. Consider this metaphor: I envision all of us to be like plants growing in a garden. We look different physically and maybe the flowers don't think they have anything in common with the ornamental grasses. But we are all manifestations of the same garden; we all get our nourishment from the same source. We all are created from and eventually return to that same source—in this example, the earth.

In my analogy the earth is consciousness; it exists within us and we can connect to it by going inward. It exists all around us, too. Yet despite our connection within the garden (whether we're flowers, perennials, annuals, grasses or vegetables), we often don't perceive our bond and when we feel alone, we forget our commonality. That, in turn, makes us feel even lonelier. But just because we may fail to perceive our unity with the other plants and the garden as a whole, are we disconnected? The answer is no. Even when we aren't conscious of the relationship we share with one another and the source, we are still attached. However, when we realize it, we feel a sense of harmony. When we recognize our true condition, we can calm our anxiety of being a lone flower and draw energy and sustenance from the source. We feel better when we are aware of our place within the whole garden, nourish ourselves (through spiritual practice) and don't feel so isolated.

Sometimes we forget that we are even in a garden. Maybe it's winter. The ground is covered in snow and we don't understand that beneath the blanket of white lies a dormant garden. We don't perceive it, yet the garden is teeming with potential. But as spring arrives and the sun melts the snow, greenery starts to sprout and we see that the fertility was there all along.

It is the same when we go outside and it's a cloudy winter day. Is the sun gone all winter? Of course not. Even in the midst of the worst storm, it is hanging right above us as always, just concealed behind a shroud of clouds. Sometimes we can see the sun and sometimes we can't. Sometimes we feel more connected to one another and our source and sometimes we don't. When you think you are alone, helpless and fragile, then you feel more vulnerable; you forget to connect to the other plants (that is, your support system).

But more critically, you forget to draw on the nourishment and energy of your source (God, Buddha, Christ, Creative Intelligence,

Higher Consciousness). Your spiritual practices, whether praying, attending religious services, meditating or dancing in the moonlight, are your way of connecting to the garden; they will rejuvenate and ground you. This is an important step in healing and staying healthy. In the case of Maria, she was able to make use of her spirituality and religious faith in a troubled time to help her weather the hardship of loss and to heal. But even if you perceive yourself to be that lone blade of grass beaten down in a winter of postpartum depression, this challenge can be the opening for your spiritual exploration.

Religious faith and spirituality can provide a dose of prevention, too. If you take care of yourself and use your resources, including your spiritual practices, you are more centered and able to deal with problems—or just your day-to-day hassles. Spiritual tools help you navigate the road of life. Connect to the garden in whatever way you chose and you will not only heal from depression but also transform into a more vital, energetic you, ready to take on life's challenges.

Throughout this book, we have been exploring how to move out of a hopeless state of despair and change your thinking from the narrow one of depression to a broader one of life's possibilities. In some sense, you need to shift your perspective: to become inspired, to find some personal meaning and to tap into a reservoir of energy to do the work and make the changes necessary for healing and personal growth. I hope that through self-exploration, therapy, spiritual practices and a support network you can do that.

I have provided some suggestions for your healing (see chapter 8, "Principle I: Finding Ways to Heal"), but now feel free to collect your own. I encourage you to take time to reflect on your experience of postpartum depression. I urge you to search for the "cause" of your illness beyond those hormonal or biological/genetic propensities that are certainly part of the condition. When you stop looking at yourself as a victim of postpartum depression and instead see your responsibility, then you will feel more in control and empowered. When you make this cognitive shift, you will realize that this is an opportunity to change, to transform from the old you to a new, improved you. Be prepared to gain something life-enhancing from your experience of postpartum illness!

I'm not talking about wishful thinking or make-believe. I have seen my clients undergo amazing, almost magical, transformations over the years. There is a ripple effect with change; each person affects those closest to her. When a mother changes, it affects her husband or partner, their baby and all the other children. And then they undergo changes, too. Each nuclear family, in turn, has an influence on its extended family, friends, neighbors and coworkers. Likewise, this can affect the larger community. It's much like throwing a pebble into water: Though the impact is strongest next to the stone, waves continue to ripple throughout the water.

The most remarkable thing is the way *you* can morph into a new, improved self through an experience like postpartum depression. Open your mind to believe that it's possible. Otherwise, you will remain in a dark place of misery and hopelessness. Too many women (and their families) have seen tragedy from thinking they could never get better, that they were somehow stuck for the long haul in that miserable world of depression. So it starts with you. Can you imagine that you will get better—not just healthy but better than you were before your illness? I'm here to tell you that it's not just a possibility; it's a certainty, if you can only imagine it.

I visited Strawberry Fields, the John Lennon memorial in New York's Central Park. Seeing the "Imagine" mosaic at its heart made me think about the way that change starts by imagining it. Then eventually it becomes a new reality. Can you imagine being different? One of the most powerful messages I can impart here is to urge you to be open to transformation, to consider the possibility that through this challenge you will change. I'm not saying it's easy. However, this intense experience *will* affect you in *some* profound way. Let that impact be a positive one. As you move through the struggle, be aware that something important can be learned. Your job is to find its meaning for yourself, to integrate it and use it to move forward as a wiser, healthier woman. Transformations follow from overcoming challenges in your life and this postpartum period qualifies as a major challenge.

# CHAPTER 12

## *Principle IV: The Healing Effect of Your Narrative*

Finding meaning, which is a blend of processing your postpartum depression, accepting the lost expectations of a "perfect" perinatal event and discovering something significant in your experience, often culminates in talking with others about what you went through. This final step is vital, but it has rarely been addressed as part of the healing process. When you ignore this phase of recovery, what's left is a sense of shame in the illness and its utter futility. Many women who fail to find meaning in their conditions attempt to hide their struggles. They are ashamed to tell their family, friends or others what they went through. These women may ultimately lack a sense of empowerment and end up feeling low self-esteem or defining themselves as defective or damaged.

Throughout this book, you have read the incredible stories of brave women who have suffered through this illness and have found new meaning, which has had a remarkable effect on the course of their lives. This is not to say that every woman I have treated could recount a similar tale. Many stay in psychotherapy only long enough to get relief from their symptoms or to complete the first two phases of the healing process. That's a choice I respect. However, when someone is willing to follow through on all the phases, more often than not the result is tremendously satisfying personal growth and change. As a therapist, I know that this is an amazing process to witness. I feel honored and extremely lucky to be a part of this process and for it to be my life's work.

The final step in the recovery process is finding meaning, which occurs once a woman works through her postpartum depression experience. This requires a woman to grieve the loss of the way it was "supposed" to be and accept her less-than-perfect experience. Women who are willing to do this may feel sad and mourn the quality time they never spent with their babies, moments that are gone forever. I still feel unhappy when I look at old pictures of myself holding my infant son, aware that I was physically present but emotionally detached and joyless. The best we can do is accept things and know that we have grown and gained something significant from our experiences. This makes all the difference between being stuck in regret and moving on, accepting that it's a loss and dealing with it. This kind of acceptance and working through difficulties helps women to be more than just asymptomatic—they become more whole and fully recovered.

Women who are willing to discuss their postpartum depression openly seem to have a better outcome than those who are ashamed. Many of my clients say they don't want anyone but their husbands to know they've had this condition; some are adamant that no one find out what they went through. This is where people can become stuck: They have just endured an intense experience and want so badly to put it all behind them and be "normal." Sometimes this reaction comes from a fear they'll be judged as unstable or bad mothers. They are worried what friends and relatives will think, that they'll be compared to people with extreme cases of postpartum illness, like Andrea Yates, a mother who took the lives of her five children during an episode of postpartum psychosis. Others just want to forget it ever happened, not think about it, talk about it or be reminded of it. It's frightening for recovering women to remember their vulnerability and realize they could fall prey to future episodes of depression. Some are even afraid that just thinking about their depression and the way it felt could cause a relapse. Recuperating women typically exclaim: "I never want to get back to that point."

What is the purpose of telling your story? By nature, human beings are storytellers. We use tales or myths to organize disparate bits of information and to express ourselves to others. Some of the earliest myth-making is evident in the rudimentary symbols and drawings scratched onto cave walls thousands of years ago in places like Lascaux, France. Regardless of their form—spoken, carved, painted or written—stories have had an important role in human history and communication for millennia.

As the French existentialist Jean-Paul Sartre says in his novel *Nausea*, "a man is always a teller of tales; he lives surrounded by his stories and the stories of others, he sees everything that happens to him through them; and he tries to live his own life as if he were telling a story."[1]

In the book *The Stories We Live By*, author and psychologist Dan McAdams writes, "If you want to know me, then you must know my story, for my story defines who I am." He continues, "If *I* want to know *myself*, to gain insight into the meaning of my own life, then I, too, must come to know my own story." We each try to understand our confusing experiences with a sense of coherence by composing "a heroic narrative of the self that illustrates essential truths about ourselves," McAdams adds. His theory is that we come to know who we are through the act of creating this story of the self. There are various kinds of stories, each with a different purpose. Some even help us to mend, McAdams says, and can "move us toward psychological fulfillment and maturity."[2]

"Storytelling is in our blood. It is part of our nature," Robert Atkinson writes in his book *The Gift of Stories: Practical and Spiritual Applications of Autobiography, Life Stories, and Personal Mythmaking*. People have been sharing their own narratives since the beginning of language. "Putting our life's events into the form of a story," Atkinson continues, "can help us bear a burden or see with a clearer perspective."[3]

When a client begins therapy or a support group, I ask her to tell me her story. There is something therapeutic about organizing your thoughts into a narrative and then hearing yourself speak the words aloud to another person. Conversely, when a client recounts the tale of her life or of a particular time frame or situation, it allows the therapist to process with her a shared experience that's unique to the client. Any time you listen to someone's story, you get to feel a bit of that other person, a sense of who she is and what she has been through.

Although telling your story to a friend, a relative or even a fellow sufferer in a support group is different from relating it to your therapist, all these situations have significant value. In each case, you are conveying the sequence of events that represents your experience. That helps to clear your mind, sort out the order of events and gain perspective. Verbal communication is not the only way to chronicle your story, though; women often find it helpful to write it down and many therapists recommend that clients keep a journal as a therapeutic tool.

Women also indicate frequently that sharing their experiences with other women in support groups and receiving validation can be enormously healing. It's amazing to see how closely and rapidly these participants bond. I have facilitated postpartum support groups for more than fourteen years and have seen members develop strong connections with virtual strangers within a few weeks. As women recount their stories and feel accepted rather than judged, they expose themselves and allow others to witness their vulnerability. This effect is not limited to support groups; discussing your postpartum experience openly with others can be exceedingly beneficial regardless of the setting.

As women talk about their perinatal time periods, they begin to deal with not only the specific events they went through but also their previous expectations as compared with the reality of their not quite "perfect" postpartum experiences. This allows them to cope with their various losses and they begin to grieve the time that was missed in less than ideal experiences.

It's unclear whether talking about your postpartum episode is a technique for healing, evidence of the healing process or a sign that you have worked through your experience and come to accept it. Perhaps it's all three. According to the National Storytelling Network, relating and listening to stories has powerful healing effects, which is why it's been essential to the work of therapists, clergy and healthcare practitioners of all kinds. Possibly when you relate your story, it gives you the unique opportunity to stand back and evaluate what was significant. Whatever the reason, there is something in the process of telling one's tale that seems to be inherently therapeutic and an important final step that hasn't been focused on previously as part of the curative process.

This reminds me of a client of mine who was uncomfortable having anyone know about her postpartum anxiety.

---

### Amy's Story

*Amy started therapy shortly after delivering her first baby, hoping to address her acute anxiety and panic attacks and the obsessive thought that someone would hurt her child. Because she worried uncontrollably about her baby's safety and had difficulty trusting others, she never wanted to leave the infant with a sitter or even a family member. She did everything herself, accepting very little help, and as a result was "bone tired" and depleted. This exhausted state made her more vulnerable to anxiety, panic attacks and a depressed mood. Over the course of treatment, she began to heal her anxious and depressive symptoms but was left with an enormous amount of guilt and shame over her postpartum experience.*

*Even after Amy became asymptomatic, she did not feel good about herself. Although she had always been outgoing, she started to withdraw from social interactions out of a sense of shame, which was eroding her self-concept and self-esteem. Less contact with friends also meant avoiding questions about her postpartum experience, which she was incredibly uncomfortable discussing. Because she didn't talk about the depression, she was unable to become more comfortable with it. That left her feeling like she had a shameful secret. It began to drive a wedge between Amy and her friends and family.*

*Without real-world feedback, Amy began to assume that "if anyone found out they would think badly of me." She even told herself that others might not want her around their children, something particularly painful in that she was a devoted teacher and loved children.*

*After having a second baby and another postpartum depression period, Amy finally agreed to attend a support group meeting, even though she was still reluctant to talk to family or friends about her thoughts and emotions.*

*At the meeting, she found it enormously helpful to tell her story and meet other women who were suffering from similar postpartum experiences. This helped Amy transform the way she viewed herself: from a damaged, despicable person to a survivor of an incredibly hard time. Her perception of herself began to change as she finally accepted the fact that she had been clinging to irrational beliefs for years. Slowly she reconnected with friends and spoke more freely about what she had gone through those first few months of her babies' lives. Most impressive, however, has been Amy's evolution from self-loathing to confident, which continues as she retells her story to others.*

---

## TELL YOUR STORY

Are you like Amy? Has your postpartum depression left you full of shame and self-loathing? Are you embarrassed to talk openly about your experience? When you think back to the first months or year of your baby's life, does it make you feel profoundly sad—or empowered and stronger? If you are ashamed or embarrassed, you have not healed completely.

Postpartum depression needn't be—nor should it be—a dirty little secret. It's important to start telling others what you have gone through. I'm not suggesting you stop people in the supermarket and bend their ear. Just speak more openly with your friends and family or join a postpartum support group. It's the difference between shame and empowerment. This illness doesn't have to be a negative event that continues to wear away your self-image and self-esteem. It could be a crucible, the significant life event that forges your confidence and renders you stronger than ever.

We often gain a new perspective when we step back from an event. Jon Kabat-Zinn, author of the book *Wherever You Go, There You Are,* has written that although at the outset of a journey we have no idea where our path will lead or how we will fare, later we are often able to trace the passage from its beginning and see how everything has come together and helped us to grow.

As time passes and your postpartum depression is further behind you, you may become aware of various changes that have resulted from your experience. Write down your personal narrative of postpartum depression, using as much detail as possible. Did depression begin immediately after delivery or did the symptoms start earlier, during pregnancy? When did you know that you were not acting like yourself? What were the signs? How did you find help? Include as many specifics as possible to describe your postpartum episode and the surrounding events that may have contributed to it.

Include not only factual details but also ways in which you have changed: How have you grown? What have you learned? Has this condition affected your intimate relationships? How has this condition transformed you? If you can't answer these questions right now, that's okay. Each woman has her own account. Whether it's similar to the ones we've discussed in this book or vastly different, it is unique. One day you will be ready to rewrite your story of postpartum depression from a fresh point of view, with an unexpected ending.

---

### In Her Own Words: Sara's Story

*"It's a girl!" the doctor exclaimed, holding the baby in the air for me to see. "Would you like to hold her?" As I embraced my newborn, I could not believe I had given birth to this beautiful child. My husband tried to capture her every movement with a video camera; the new daddy was beaming. Our dream of becoming parents had finally come true. We had a healthy baby and she was precious. We could not wait to bring her home and introduce her to our family and friends. Weeks went by*

*and we loved playing and caring for our bundle of joy. Everything seemed perfect.*

*Then one afternoon, while cradling my baby, tears dripped uncontrollably down my cheeks and I felt extreme sadness. I wondered what was wrong with me. I could not understand why I was so depressed when I should have been overjoyed. Day after day this crying continued and I was confused about my emotions. I absolutely loved my daughter but could not stop feeling depressed. At the same time, I became obsessed with worrying about my daughter and had terrible thoughts that something or someone might harm her. I became engulfed in a fog of despair. Even today it's difficult to reflect on those dark hours when I wept. I had no idea I was going through postpartum depression.*

*When I visited my doctor for a six-week postpartum checkup, she didn't mention the possibility of depression, so I didn't share how I was feeling. As my days became more difficult, I spoke to my mom about my emotions. She told me she'd had postpartum depression after my brother's birth and needed to see a psychologist. I was scared by the mere thought of having this condition and worried that I was becoming crazy. I went to a therapist who asked me questions about how I felt, which scared me even more. She asked if I wanted to harm my baby. Harm my baby? I thought to myself. Why would she ask that? My anxiety elevated. I tried to focus on the rest of her questions, but her words became faint. I quickly exited her office at the end of the session and never returned.*

*I called my physician many times about what I was going through. I spoke to various nurses until the physician finally spoke with me. She was surprisingly uncomfortable discussing postpartum depression and quickly referred me to another psychologist. I hung up and felt a whirlwind of emotions. I was hurt and angry by the doctor's reaction. I also felt ashamed that I was so miserable when I should have been exuberant. I decided to give one more psychologist a try.*

*This time I went to a mental health professional who specialized in postpartum depression and understood what was happening to me. Through therapy I learned more about the disorder and developed coping strategies and hope for a happier future. I also went to a psychiatrist who prescribed an antidepressant to stabilize my obsessive thoughts and modify my depressed state. It took many months, but I slowly began to feel better, less anxious and more at peace. I took pleasure once again in being with my baby and didn't worry about her obsessively. I started to feel like myself and saw my way through those foggy days. It was not an easy process and I occasionally had setbacks. But with the support of my family and therapist, I was finally able to enjoy my dream of being a mommy.*

*My oldest daughter is now six and I am the proud mother of three wonderful girls. I went through postpartum depression after each of my pregnancies, but the experiences were not as frightening during the second two; I had the continued support of my family and therapist and took antidepressants after the births. My obsessive thoughts became manageable and I was better equipped to cope with the condition.*

*Sharing my story is not easy, for it brings back memories of great despair. But it also reminds me of how I triumphed over difficult times and grew stronger from my experiences. Going through postpartum depression has helped me reflect on my past and understand myself better. I learned that many of my struggles during these periods relate to my personality and need for perfection. While I was in high school and college, my obsession was getting the best scores on all exams, papers and projects. I was an extremely diligent student and developed great anxiety while striving for straight As on my report cards. My thoughts and focus were constantly on receiving perfect grades and proving to myself that I was smart.*

*When I first began my career in the field of education, I became obsessed with perfection as a teacher. I worked long hours outside of school to prepare the most beneficial lessons. I wanted to prove to myself that I was a superior teacher. After a couple of years, I developed self-confidence in my job and was able to enjoy it without obsessing about perfection.*

*As a young adult, I became obsessed with my weight and having the perfect figure. I was never really heavy, but I decided to join a health club to "get in shape." Unfortunately, I took this to the extreme and wandered down a destructive path, eating an ultra-low-fat diet and exercising intensely. What began as an effort to better my health ended as an eating disorder. It wasn't until I developed amenorrhea (i.e., I stopped menstruating) that I realized I was taking "getting in shape" too far. As a result, when I decided to get pregnant (with my first daughter), I needed fertility treatments.*

*While pregnant, I no longer obsessed about my body, but rather about the little body I was caring for inside me. My new obsession was her health and wellness. After my first daughter was born, I assumed these obsessive thoughts would be over, because I was with her and able to care for her. And I seemed to be doing well—until a fellow teacher called to tell me that a recent student of mine had died over the summer in an accident. He was only five years old and I was devastated. After that, I became obsessed about caring for my baby and I embarked on another path of anxiety while striving for perfection. I wanted to be the perfect mom and was very concerned something would happen to my own child.*

*Going through therapy for postpartum depression has helped me understand my past struggles and the theme of perfectionism that has permeated my life. I am now better equipped to handle anxiety and depression. The right combination of talk therapy, medication and personal support helps me persevere. The obsessive thoughts have eased and I am more at peace in my mind. Over the years I have also become more self-confident in my role as a mother. I realize that perfectionism does not bring happiness and I can be a wonderful mom without needing to be the best.*

---

Sara's healing work focused on her unrealistically high expectations, the need to be in control and issues of perfectionism. She often pushed herself to the limit of exhaustion trying to do it all and to do things perfectly. Her struggle to be a "superwoman" and "supermom" created enormous anxiety. She strived to excel in everything and, despite her accomplishments, she was never quite good enough.

Initially, I provided education about postpartum depression to decrease Sara's fear about the anxiety she was experiencing as well as to give her some sense of control and empowerment, both critically important when facing depression. In treatment, Sara worked on identifying her coping skills, changing her "all-or-nothing" thinking (seeing things in black and white extremes leads one to feel that anything less than perfect is a failure) and being more self-compassionate. Sara's unrealistic standards were a part of distorted and unrealistic thinking that had set her up for a fall. She had to unlearn these maladaptive perfectionist ideas and replace them with more manageable realistic ones by striving to be "good enough" rather than perfect.

As she grew more insightful and learned new skills during our therapeutic journey, Sara moved forward and began finding the path to a satisfying, realistic life in which she trusted herself to be a good mother.

# CHAPTER 13

## *Post-Postpartum Transitions and Transformations*

Things are not always what they seem, as evidenced by the women's stories in this book. When we are faced with a particularly painful experience or period in our lives, we often ask, why is this happening to me? It's an existential question I hear frequently from new clients. Though I cannot answer it at the start of therapy, I try to reassure clients that they will eventually understand the *why* themselves. Often they also gain something valuable from their experiences. However, many clients cannot take comfort from that; typically, they're so immersed in their pain that they're unable to hear or perhaps to believe anything positive can emerge.

I have focused on some of the valuable life lessons that can occur as a result of postpartum depression. The women who shared their stories and those in the case studies I describe are a small sample of the mothers I have treated over the years. There are so many more incredible accounts, but I've had to limit myself to a few who characterize the inner strength, survival drive, tremendous personal growth and enriched, meaningful life that this illness can inspire. Sometimes in a book of this kind, you get a snapshot of someone during a difficult transition. At the time, the person doesn't know that her experience will change the course of her life and ultimately enrich it. These are the stories I present; they portray women just like you. It is my intent to provide the hope and inspiration that can be difficult to find on your own. I encourage you to allow your story to unfold so that at some point you, too, will know what a positive effect your illness can have.

As you read this book I am sure that you've thought a lot about your own experience of postpartum depression. Each woman going through this illness faces similar symptoms, yet the lessons each acquires are unique. Even if the overall symptoms look alike, the environmental factors, hormonal sensitivity and biological vulnerability that led to the illness often differ from one woman to the next.

Take some time now to think about what contributed to your own condition. What made you vulnerable to depression during this period? Consider these questions and answer them honestly:

- Do you have a large support network of friends and/or relatives whom you can call on for help—or just a few individuals?
- Do you have ways of coping during stressful times?
- Is your primary relationship with your spouse or partner satisfying?
- Do you feel loved and respected?
- Can you ask for help or do you try to do everything yourself?
- Do you feel guilty when you take time for yourself?
- Are you exhausted from years of poor health habits, like insufficient sleep, lack of exercise and an unhealthy diet?
- Do you often find yourself taking care of others' needs but neglecting your own?
- Do you avoid change and have trouble adjusting to new situations?
- Can you laugh at yourself and maintain a sense of humor in stressful times?
- Do you take life too seriously?
- Do you buy into the myth of the "supermom"?
- Are you a perfectionist?
- Are you a people-pleaser?

- Do you compare yourself with others?
- Do you think everyone else is better and more "together" than you are?
- Are you self-critical and hard on yourself?
- Do you have trouble taking time to relax?
- Do you live by a to-do list?
- Do you take on too much or have difficultly saying no?
- Do you know how to have fun and make time for recreational activities?

Do some of these questions strike a familiar chord? They all address issues that can make you more vulnerable to anxiety and depression. The good news is that while they are concerns, they are not, in and of themselves, diseases. You can work on them alone or with your therapist. To create a personal list, write down your own issues, noting any behaviors that could be problematic and then answering the questions as candidly as possible.

When you are finished, review the list you have written. Then write down your answers to these next questions:

- What other life events may have contributed?
- What have you learned about yourself?

Hopefully, doing this exercise and reflecting upon your personal episode of postpartum depression will help you learn a lot about yourself. But remember: In order to find meaning in your experience, you may need to be symptom-free and further along in the healing process. Does that describe you? If so, take some time to consider and write down your answers to this next set of self-reflective questions:

- Why do you think you developed postpartum depression?
- How have you changed as a result of having postpartum depression?
- How have you grown as an individual?
- What have you learned about yourself or about life in general?

I know this is an incredibly painful and challenging period. But it's also one ripe with potential for enormous growth. Like the women whose stories you've read in this book, you have been through perhaps the worst of times. Yet out of that experience and eventual recovery comes meaning and a new beginning.

At the end of chapter 12, I urged you to write down your postpartum tale. Now I suggest you retell your story from a fresh perspective, incorporating all you've learned about yourself and your illness from the exercises, strategies and advice you've employed. Most of all, in the journey we've undertaken together, I hope you have learned to reflect upon your own feelings about the past that have brought you to this day and the future you want to create. Title your new story "My Post-Postpartum Depression Metamorphosis." After you compose your narrative, I hope you will send it to my blog at http://post-postpartumdepressionblog.com to inspire others.

Your struggle with postpartum depression is likely not the first—nor will it be the last—challenge you will face. The longer we live, the more tests we confront. No one is immune to life's troubles and difficult situations. But you have an opportunity to tackle and defeat your postpartum illness. It's these very circumstances that force us to stretch beyond our comfort zones and it all starts with a shift in thinking, from impossible to possible.

# CONCLUSION

Transformation is what this book is about. It is a challenge to turn postpartum depression into a positive life-altering experience. Women going through its intensity want the suffering to be finished. Many clients come to their initial appointments feeling impatient for relief and desiring to get back to their old selves. We are brought up to be goal-focused in our society, so it's understandable that you only want to get to the end of the misery.

Often, clients question me about how long the process will take. They want me to wave a magic wand or prescribe some antidote that will take away the pain and change everything. They want to be symptom free and to feel like themselves again. These women do not realize the growth potential. And yet the journey between the two endpoints is where all the changes take place.

Unfortunately it's not simple; there is no effortless wisdom that will miraculously make you well. It is a process of our working together, directing our efforts to figuring out what helps and discovering what meaning you can take away from your experience. The process itself—or perhaps the pain—makes you reflect, stretch and somehow change from who you were when the illness began. However, the personal journey through postpartum disorder you have to take is a test of strength and persistence, a major life challenge that will alter you in ways you never imagined. You cannot move through such an intense illness and just go back to being your "old self." Nor would you want to, because you would miss the opportunity for real transformation. Instead, you should expect to grow from this experience and become a changed person—someone different from who you were when it all began.

From time to time we all encounter what seem like insurmountable odds. Some problems *feel* like they're undefeatable because we *think* they're impossible to overcome. But that's nonsense. I know it. I've been there many times, as I'm sure you have, too. My mind now goes to some of those earlier rough patches—for instance, when I suffered from postpartum depression myself. As challenging as that was, it also engendered some of the most incredible changes in my life.

Your struggle with postpartum depression is likely not the first challenge you will face—nor will it be the last. The longer we live, the more tests we confront. No one is immune to life's troubles and difficult situations. But you have a chance now to tackle and defeat your postpartum illness, just as I did. It's these very circumstances that force us to stretch beyond our comfort zones and it all starts with a shift in thinking, from impossible to possible. How can you overcome this illness and transform yourself? How can you give meaning to your experience of postpartum depression and create something positive in its place?

Women struggling with postpartum depression need an understanding of the illness itself, which helps defuse their fears while maintaining the hope that they can heal and return to pre-pregnancy functioning, at the very least. I've laid out many of the facts, provided an overview of the illness and differentiated between normal postpartum adjustment and the various postpartum mood and anxiety disorders.

Although you may want to believe that depression is all about hormones and brain chemistry, that is only part of the story. While many women with postpartum depression tend to be extremely sensitive to the significant drop in hormones that follows delivery, other risk factors, which we discussed earlier, such as biological vulnerability to depression and anxiety, can also play key roles. Postpartum depression is multifaceted and complex; there are multiple reasons why women experience it and these vary from person to person.

Your ultimate challenge is to find a purpose for your illness and transform whatever needs altering in your life. In accepting your struggle as a learning opportunity, you can make these changes and inspire yourself to recover and grow.

I focused on four principles that are necessary in order to get well, grow and find personal meaning or significance through postpartum depression. The first principle is to find various tools and interventions for healing the depression and/or anxiety. These might include exercising, taking nutritional supplements, setting small, manageable goals for yourself, finding balance and using full-spectrum light bulbs in your home and office. In individual psychotherapy, clients and I examine their concerns together and apply various techniques while we figure out what contributed to their illness and what changes they need to make to get better. It starts out as a mystery, but in time we put the pieces together and solve the puzzle. I hope the suggestions for coping strategies I outlined will be a good starting point for you to discuss healing methods with your own therapist, physician or mental health professional. For those of you not in counseling, the list will hopefully serve as a guide to some of the resources that are available and the ways that therapists work with clients to help them fight depression and anxiety.

The second principle is the power of hope. This is a critical ingredient in the initial stage of postpartum depression, when symptoms are intense and women have to resist the despair and hopelessness that can accompany this early phase of the illness. In maintaining faith that you will not only get well but also surpass your previous level of functioning, you will continue to strive for positive mental health rather than give in to despondency.

The third principle is the power of spirituality and religion in healing. Many women with postpartum depression find that spiritual practices and religious traditions comfort them and provide positive therapeutic effects. I have presented some of the results of the wide range of scientific studies that support these claims: research done at prestigious universities and reported in reputable medical journals which confirms that integrative medicine—that is, alternative and faith-based practices used in conjunction with traditional medicine—aids in the treatment of mind, body and spirit. This whole-person approach seems to enhance the effectiveness of medical care for many illnesses, from cancer and heart disease to depression.

Religious faith and spirituality can heal your depression and help you cope with life's difficulties by connecting you to the world beyond your five senses—a spiritual reality. It can also help you maintain good mental health by providing a dose of prevention. Any ritual, belief or spiritual practice that offers relief, directs self-reflection and helps you to heal can aid in your recovery and transformation. Making changes, growing and finding personal meaning in this experience are what it's all about.

The fourth principle is sharing your story. Once healing is underway and symptoms have become less intense—perhaps they've even remitted partially or in full—women are often struck by the discrepancy between the perfect postpartum life they expected to share with their newborns and the actual experiences they had. This is often accompanied by sadness and a sense of disappointment and loss, which needs to be accepted and worked through in order to recover fully without leaving a residue of shame.

Sometimes women need to grieve the lost time and mourn their own less-than-perfect perinatal experiences. It can be particularly healing for women to talk about their postpartum depression with other women: friends, relatives or moms in a support group. Instead of expressing themselves verbally, some women prefer writing or journaling as a means of working out their feelings and conveying their stories. These are all equally beneficial. Women who are more open and willing to work through their feelings seem to have better outcomes and are generally left with better self-regard and positive senses of self for having survived such extremely difficult periods.

I hope that this book has given you needed information and tools to take on your journey to wellness. More than that, my aim has been to inspire you and show you a different perspective on postpartum depression, one that is more life-affirming. I am confident that this will encourage you to shift your focus from a victim to someone who has been offered a great challenge: overcoming illness and using the experience for personal growth and the path to a new, improved version of you.

In the end, the final chapter, of course, is your own. My hope is that by gaining information and learning to understand your feelings, symptoms, restorative measures and, most of all, your outlook, you can now see that your postpartum depression can be a catalyst for transformation and an opportunity to reevaluate your life choices and that it has ultimately led to healing and a new beginning for you.

Remember, postpartum depression is not the end of the story. It is just the beginning. Best wishes on your travels. May you enjoy positive changes and transformation.

# ACKNOWLEDGEMENTS

I especially wish to acknowledge all the amazing women whose stories appear in these pages. I am grateful to each of them for sharing their personal struggles and for reflecting honestly on the meaning of their experiences. They are truly incredible, strong women who have found happy endings—and new beginnings.

I'd also like to acknowledge my wonderful son and daughter, Seth and Hadar, who have brought meaning to my life and taught me about unconditional love and acceptance. Special thanks to my parents, who were there for me both emotionally, with their love, and physically, by coming to my home and sitting with me when I was in misery; to my sister, Linda Benjamin, who took time out from her busy life to spend countless hours on the phone with me; to my ex-husband, David Feingold, who helped as much as he could even when he didn't understand what I was going through or why I was suffering so; to my dear friend Sindy Velen Rosenberg, who, fearing that I was desperate enough to take my own life, took a plane flight cross-country to be with me when she heard I was discouraged and ready to give up.

In addition, I want to acknowledge my close friend Carol Feingold, who has given me so much support over the past few years, and Michael Jones, who gratuitously encouraged me to finish this book, allowing me to spend time alone at his farm to write without distraction.

A special thank you to the numerous professionals who have compiled lists of Web sites, phone numbers and other resources for perinatal women, many of which I have included.

Finally, I have to add a word of thanks to my amazing editor, Holly Haynes. She read through every word, making sure I wrote what I meant and meant what I wrote. I'm so appreciative to her for helping me make this a better book than the one I started with many versions ago.

And special thanks go to my literary agent, Maryann Karinch, and to all those at New Horizon Press, including Joanna, Charley, Dr. Joan Dunphy and the many others who have contributed to the publication of this book.

The love and support from all of you has enabled me to complete this endeavor and, ultimately, do the work I find so meaningful and satisfying.

# APPENDIX A

## RESOURCES FOR WOMEN, FAMILIES AND HEALTHCARE PROVIDERS

### Support Groups, Organizations and Web Sites

Here are some resources that can help you find healthcare providers and support groups in your area as well as additional information on postpartum disorders and other women's stories. The list is not intended to be exhaustive but to offer a few well-regarded starting places. (Please note: All phone numbers are for business purposes only unless otherwise indicated.)

**American Psychiatric Association (APA)**
http://www.psych.org
1000 Wilson Boulevard, Suite 182
Arlington, VA 22209
888-35-PSYCH (77924)

**American Psychological Association (APA)**
http://www.apa.org
750 First Street NE
Washington, DC 20002-4242
800-374-2721

**Anxiety Disorders Association of America (ADAA)**
http://www.adaa.org
8701 Georgia Ave., Suite 412
Silver Spring, MD 20910
240-485-1001

**Central New Jersey Maternal and Child Health Consortium (CNJMCHC)**
http://www.cnjmchc.org
2 King Arthur Court, Suite B
North Brunswick, NJ 08902
732-937-5437
and
725 Airport Road, Suite 1C
Lakewood, NJ 08701
732-363-5400

**Emory Women's Mental Health Program**
http://womensmentalhealth.emory.edu
Emory University School of Medicine
Emory Clinic Building B
1365 Clifton Road NE, Suite 6100
Atlanta, GA 30322
404-778-2524
This program, affiliated with Emory University, focuses on the evaluation and treatment of perinatal mood disorders.

**MedEdPPD.org**
http://www.mededppd.org
MedEdPPD.org was developed with the support of the National Institute of Mental Health, which is a federal government agency and part of the U.S. Department of Health and Human Services. This site offers perinatal information in English and Spanish.

**MGH Center for Women's Mental Health**
http://www.womensmentalhealth.org
Perinatal and Reproductive Psychiatry Program
Simches Research Building
185 Cambridge St Suite 2200
Boston, MA 02114
617-724-7792

**Motherrisk**
http://www.motherrisk.org
Support line: 416-813-6780, 877-439-2744
This support line, affiliated with the University of Toronto, provides information and answers questions about the risk and safety of medications for pregnant, breast-feeding and postpartum mothers.

**New Jersey Department of Health and Senior Services**
http://www.state.nj.us/health/fhs/ppd/index.shtml
Support line: 800-328-3838
This organization provides online information about perinatal mood disorders in English and Spanish, including videos, support groups throughout the state and additional links.

**NorthShore University HealthSystem**
Jennifer Mudd Houghtaling Postpartum Depression Program
http://www.northshore.org/obstetrics/perinatal-depression/
Support line: 866-364-MOMS (6667)
A free, confidential twenty-four-hour hotline for residents of Illinois, this program provides information and help in finding a therapist or support group.

**Office on Women's Health (OWH)**
The National Women's Health Information Center
http://www.womenshealth.gov
Support line: 800-994-9662
Department of Health and Human Services
200 Independence Avenue, SW Room 712E
Washington, DC 20201
202-690-7650
The Office on Women's Health is a part of the U.S. Department of Health and Human Services, an agency of the federal government. OWH provides a free help line staffed by English- and Spanish-speaking specialists, numerous publications about postpartum depression and an extensive Web site.

**Postpartum Education for Parents**
http://www.sbpep.org
Support line: 805-564-3888
PO Box 261
Santa Barbara, CA 93116

**Postpartum Progress**
http://www.postpartumprogress.typepad.com
Postpartum Progress is a blog on postpartum depression. It offers information, stories of survivors and news items as well as recommends books.

**Postpartum Resource Center of New York, Inc.**
http://www.postpartumny.org
Support line: 631-422-2255, 855-631-0001
109 Udall Road
West Islip, NY 11795

**Postpartum Stressline**
Support line: 888-678-2669
This call center is staffed with trained volunteers who are survivors of postpartum depression.

**Postpartum Support International (PSI)**
http://www.postpartum.net
Support line: 800-944-4PPD (4773)
6706 SW 54th Avenue
Portland, Oregon 97219
503-894-9453
PSI is a worldwide nonprofit organization "dedicated to helping women who are suffering from Perinatal Mood & Anxiety Disorders, including postpartum depression, the most common complication of childbirth." The group offers information, connection to coordinators throughout most of the United States and twenty-six other countries and English- and Spanish-language support.

**The Post-Postpartum Depression Blog**
http://post-postpartumdepressionblog.com/

**Ruth Rhoden Craven Foundation, Inc., for Postpartum Depression Awareness**
http://www.ppdsupport.org
This nonprofit organization provides information and support for women with postpartum depression and their families.

## PERINATAL MOOD AND ANXIETY

### Books and Articles

*Anxiety in Childbearing Women: Diagnosis and Treatment* by Amy Wenzel

"A Checklist to Identify Women at Risk for Developing Postpartum Depression" by Cheryl Tatano Beck (*Journal of Obstetric, Gynecologic, and Neonatal Nursing*)

*The Cinderella Syndrome: When the Glass Slipper No Longer Fits* by Tann Moore

*The Cradle Will Fall* by Carl S. Burak and Michele G. Remington

*A Daughter's Touch* by Sylvia M. Lasalandra

*Depression after Childbirth: How to Recognise, Treat, and Prevent Postnatal Depression* by Katherina Dalton and Wendy Holton

*Depression in New Mothers: Causes, Consequences, and Treatment Alternatives* by Kathleen A. Kendall-Tackett

*Down Came the Rain: My Journey through Postpartum Depression* by Brooke Shields

*Evaluation and Treatment of Postpartum Emotional Disorders* by Ann L. Dunnewold

*Mood and Anxiety Disorders During Pregnancy and Postpartum* edited by Lee S. Cohen and Ruta M. Nonacs

*The Mother-to-Mother Postpartum Depression Support Book* by Sandra Poulin

*Mothering the New Mother: Women's Feelings and Needs after Childbirth* by Sally Placksin

"Obsessions and Compulsions in Women with Postpartum Depression" by Katherine L. Wisner, Kathleen S. Peindl, Thomas Gigliotti and Barbara H. Hanusa (*Journal of Clinical Psychiatry*)

*Perinatal and Postpartum Mood Disorders: Perspectives and Treatment Guide for the Health Care Practitioner* edited by Susan Dowd Stone and Alexis E. Menken

*Postpartum Depression: Case Studies, Research, and Nursing Care* by Cheryl Tatano Beck

*Postpartum Depression: A Comprehensive Approach for Nurses* by Kathleen A. Kendall-Tackett and Glenda Kaufman Kantor

*Postpartum Depression: Every Woman's Guide to Diagnosis, Treatment, and Prevention* by Sharon L. Roan

"Postpartum Depression: Midwives' Expanding Role" by Susan Benjamin Feingold (*Birth Gazette*)

*Postpartum Depression Demystified: An Essential Guide for Understanding and Overcoming the Most Common Complication after Childbirth* by Joyce A. Venis and Suzanne McCloskey

*Postpartum Depression for Dummies* by Shoshana S. Bennett and Mary Jo Codey

*Postpartum Psychiatric Illness: A Picture Puzzle* by James Alexander Hamilton and Patricia Neel Harberger

*Postpartum Survival Guide* by Ann Dunnewold and Diane G. Sanford

*Shouldn't I Be Happy? Emotional Problems of Pregnant and Postpartum Women* by Shaila Misri

*Therapy and the Postpartum Woman: Notes on Healing Postpartum Depression for Clinicians and the Women Who Seek Their Help* by Karen R. Kleiman

*This Isn't What I Expected: Overcoming Postpartum Depression* by Karen R. Kleiman and Valerie Raskin

*When Words Are Not Enough: The Women's Prescription for Depression and Anxiety* by Valerie Raskin

*Women's Moods: What Every Woman Must Know about Hormones, the Brain, and Emotional Health* by Deborah Sichel and Jeanne W. Driscoll

*The Yellow Wall-Paper, Herland, and Selected Writings* by Charlotte Perkins Gilman

## SPIRITUALITY

### Books

*The Age of Miracles: Embracing the New Midlife* by Marianne Williamson

*Attitudes of Gratitude: How to Give and Receive Joy Every Day of Your Life* by M. J. Ryan

*Being in Balance: 9 Principles for Creating Habits to Match Your Desires* by Wayne Dyer

*Broken Open: How Difficult Times Can Help Us Grow* by Elizabeth Lesser

*Chi: Discovering Your Life Energy* by Waysun Liao

*Creative Visualization: Use the Power of Your Imagination to Create What You Want in Your Life* by Shakti Gawain

*Each Day a New Beginning: Daily Meditations for Women* a Hazelden Meditation Series

*Fire in the Soul: A New Psychology of Spiritual Optimism* by Joan Borysenko

*Flourish: A Visionary New Understanding of Happiness and Well-being* by Martin E. P. Seligman

*God Is Not a Christian, Nor a Jew, Muslim, Hindu . . . : God Dwells With Us, In Us, Around Us, As Us* by Carlton Pearson

*The Happiness Project: Or, Why I Spent a Year Trying to Sing in the Morning, Clean My Closets, Fight Right, Read Aristotle, and Generally Have More Fun* by Gretchen Rubin

*How Good Do We Have to Be? A New Understanding of Guilt and Forgiveness* by Harold S. Kushner

*The Intimate Life: Awakening to the Spiritual Essence in Yourself and Others* by Judith Blackstone

*A Lamp in the Darkness: Illuminating the Path Through Difficult Times* by Jack Kornfield

*Learned Optimism: How to Change Your Mind and Your Life* by Martin Seligman

*Living a Life That Matters: Resolving the Conflict between Conscience and Success* by Harold S. Kushner

*Living in Gratitude: A Journey That Will Change Your Life* by Angeles Arrien

*The Mindfulness Revolution: Leading Psychologists, Scientists, Artists, and Mediation Teachers on the Power of Mindfulness in Daily Life* edited by Barry Boyce

*Minding the Body, Mending The Mind* by Joan Borysenko

*Modern-Day Miracles: Miraculous Moments and Extraordinary Stories from People All Over the World Whose Lives Have Been Touched by Louise L. Hay* by Louise Hay

*A New Earth: Awakening to Your Life's Purpose* by Eckhart Tolle

*The Power of Kabbalah: This Book Contains the Secrets of the Universe and the Meaning of Our Lives* by Yehuda Berg

*The Power of Now: A Guide to Spiritual Enlightenment* by Eckhart Tolle

*Power Thoughts: 365 Daily Affirmations* by Louise Hay

*Rabbi Rami Guide to God: Roadside Assistance for the Spiritual Traveler* by Rami Shapiro

*Right Here with You: Bringing Mindful Awareness into Our Relationships* edited by Andrea Miller

*The Second Journey: The Road Back to Yourself* by Joan Anderson

*The Secret* by Rhonda Byrne

*A Seeker's Guide* by Elizabeth Lesser

*The Seven Spiritual Laws of Success: A Practical Guide to the Fulfillment of Your Dreams* by Deepak Chopra

*Taking the Leap: Freeing Ourselves from Old Habits and Fears* by Pema Chödrön

*The Tao of Joy Every Day: 365 Days of Tao Living* by Derek Lin

*The Tao of Sound: Acoustic Sound Healing for the 21st Century* by Fabien Maman

*The Way: Using the Wisdom of Kabbalah for Spiritual Transformation and Fulfillment* by Michael Berg

*Wherever You Go, There You Are: Mindfulness Meditation in Everyday Life* by Jon Kabat-Zinn

*You Are Here: Discovering the Magic of the Present Moment* by Thich Nhat Hanh

*You Can Heal Your Life* by Louise Hay

*Zen Mind, Beginner's Mind: Informal Talks on Zen Meditation and Practice* by Shunryu Suzuki

## Audio

*Advancing Your Spirit: Finding Meaning in Your Life's Journey* by Wayne W. Dyer and Marianne Williamson

*Entering the Now* by Eckhart Tolle

*Finding Your Life's Purpose* by Eckhart Tolle

*Quiet Mind: A Beginner's Guide to Meditation* edited by Susan Piver

*Reiki Sleep: Reiki Music for Blissful Sleep* by Llewellyn

*Through the Open Door to the Vastness of Your True Being* by Eckhart Tolle

*Yoga* by Putumayo World Music

## DVDs

*How to Know God* by Deepak Chopra (20th Century Fox)

*Journey Into Buddhism: Dharma River* (PBS)

*Journey Into Buddhism: Prajna Earth* (PBS)

*Journey Into Buddhism: Vajra Sky Over Tibet* (PBS)

*The Secret* by Rhonda Byrne (Prime Time Productions)

*The Shift* by Wayne W. Dyer (Hay House, Inc.)

*Through the Wormhole* narrated by Morgan Freeman (Discovery/Gaiam)

*Viniyoga Therapy for Anxiety* by Gary Kraftsow (Bayview Entertainment/Widowmaker)

*What the Bleep Do We Know?!* (20th Century Fox)

## Web Sites

Beliefnet: http://www.beliefnet.com

Spirituality and Health: http://www.spiritualityhealth.com

Oprah: http://www.oprah.com/spirit/Oprahs-Best-Life-Series-Spirituality-101

# APPENDIX B

## THE FEINGOLD POSTPARTUM DEPRESSION QUICK SCREENING

This is not to be used in lieu of other validated screening tools by mental health professionals, such as the Edinburgh Scale, the Postpartum Depression Screening Scale (PDSS) or other normed assessment tools. This is a good quick reference which can be followed by the Edinburgh or the PDSS or an in-depth interview to diagnose postpartum depression.

## SCREENING

Ask: Since having your baby, do you notice that you don't feel like yourself?

- If client says no, she feels fine, like herself, *the screening is over.*
- If client says yes, she does not feel like herself, ask whether she has any of these symptoms:
  - Sleep difficulties (insomnia, difficulty getting back to sleep in the middle of the night after getting up with baby, waking earlier than she has to)

- Significant anxiety or excessive worrying
- Loss of appetite
- Lack of joy and motivation
- Obsessive or repetitive scary thoughts
- Depressed or low mood

## SCORING

If the client has *two or more* symptoms, she should be referred for evaluation. If she has only one symptom, but the symptom is obsessive thoughts, significant mood problems (depressed or seriously anxious) or lack of joy and motivation, then she may have postpartum depression and in that case, too, she should be referred.

# APPENDIX C

## THE EDINBURGH POSTNATAL DEPRESSION SCALE

As you have recently had a baby, I would like to know how you are feeling. Please CIRCLE the answer which comes closest to how you have felt *in the past 7 days,* not just how you feel today.

Here is an example:

In the past 7 days, I have felt happy.

0 Yes, all the time.
1 Yes, most of the time.
2 No, not very often.
3 No, not at all.

**In the past 7 days:**

1. I have been able to laugh and see the funny side of things.

0 Yes, all the time.
1 Yes, most of the time.
2 No, not very often.
3 No, not at all.

2. I have looked forward with enjoyment to things.

   0 Yes, all the time.
   1 Yes, most of the time.
   2 No, not very often.
   3 No, not at all.

3. I have blamed myself unnecessarily when things went wrong.

   0 Yes, all the time.
   1 Yes, most of the time.
   2 No, not very often.
   3 No, not at all.

4. I have been anxious or worried for no good reason.

   0 Yes, all the time.
   1 Yes, most of the time.
   2 No, not very often.
   3 No, not at all.

5. I have felt scared or panicky for no very good reason.

   0 Yes, all the time.
   1 Yes, most of the time.
   2 No, not very often.
   3 No, not at all.

6. Things have been getting on top of me.

   0 Yes, all the time.
   1 Yes, most of the time.
   2 No, not very often.
   3 No, not at all.

7. I have been so unhappy that I have had difficulty sleeping.

   0 Yes, all the time.
   1 Yes, most of the time.
   2 No, not very often.
   3 No, not at all.

8. I have felt sad or miserable.

    0 Yes, all the time.
    1 Yes, most of the time.
    2 No, not very often.
    3 No, not at all.

9. I have been so unhappy that I have been crying.

    0 Yes, all the time.
    1 Yes, most of the time.
    2 No, not very often.
    3 No, not at all.

10. The thought of harming myself has occurred to me.

    0 Yes, all the time.
    1 Yes, most of the time.
    2 No, not very often.
    3 No, not at all.



Translations of the scale, and guidance as to its use, may be found in Cox, J.L. & Holden, J. (2003) *Perinatal Mental Health: A Guide to the Edinburgh Postnatal Depression Scale.* London: Gaskell.

# NOTES

### *PART I: Postpartum Emotional Disorders*

CHAPTER 1: TESTING TRUTHS AND FALSEHOODS ABOUT POSTPARTUM DEPRESSION

1. John Cox, Jenifer M. Holden and Ruth Sagovsky, "Detection of Postnatal Depression: Development of the 10-Item Edinburgh Postnatal Depression Scale," *British Journal of Psychiatry* 150 (1987): 782–6.
2. Cheryl Tatano Beck and Rober K. Gable, *Postpartum Depression Screening Scale (PDSS)* (Torrance, California: Western Psychological Services, 2002).
3. Cheryl Tatano Beck, *Postpartum Depression: Case Studies, Research, and Nursing Care* (Washington, DC: Association of Women's Health, Obstetric and Neonatal Nurses, 1999).
4. Susan Dowd Stone and Alexis E. Menken, eds., *Perinatal and Postpartum Mood Disorders: Perspectives and Treatment Guide for the Health Care Practitioner* (New York: Springer Publishing Company, 2008).
5. Ibid.

CHAPTER 2: THE POSTPARTUM CONTINUUM

1. Mayo Clinic Staff, "Postpartum Depression," Mayo Foundation for Medical Education and Research, June 3, 2012, http://www.mayoclinic.com/health/postpartum-depression/DS00546.

## *PART II: Postpartum Advice, Myths and Our Significant Relationships*

### Chapter 4: Cultural Practices, Myths and Rituals

1. "Understanding Placenta Previa – the Basics," WebMD, April 19, 2012, http://www.webmd.com/baby/understanding-placenta-previa-basics.
2. Steve Friess, "Ingesting the Placenta: Is It Healthy for New Moms?" *USA Today*, July 19, 2007, http://www.usatoday.com/news/health/2007-07-18-placenta-ingestion_N.htm.
3. Ibid.
4. Atossa Araxia Abrahamian, "The Placenta Cookbook," *New York Magazine*, August 29, 2011.
5. Melissa Dahl, "Placenta Pizza? Some New Moms Try Old Rituals," MSNBC.com, December 5, 2007, http://www.msnbc.msn.com/id/22087790/ns/health-womens_health/t/placenta-pizza-some-new-moms-try-old-rituals/#.T9YAH7Xl-3o.
6. Pamela J. Surkan, Caitlin E. Kennedy, Kristen M. Hurley and Maureen M. Black, "Maternal Depression and Early Childhood Growth in Developing Countries: Systematic Review and Meta-Analysis," *Bulletin of the World Health Organization* 89 (May 2011), http://www.who.int/bulletin/volumes/89/8/11-088187/en/.
7. Laura Miller and Elizabeth LaRusso, "Preventing Postpartum Depression," *Psychiatric Clinics of North America* 34, no 1 (March 2011): 53–65.

### Chapter 5: A Supportive Guide For Spouses And Partners

1. Sandra Poulin, *The Mother-to-Mother Postpartum Depression Support Book* (New York: Berkley Books, 2006).
2. Janice H Goodman, "Paternal Postpartum Depression, Its Relationship to Maternal Postpartum Depression, and Implications for Family Health," *Journal of Advanced Nursing* 45, no. 1 (2004): 26–35.
3. Alyson Shapiro, John M. Gottman and Sybil Carrére, "The Baby and the Marriage: Identifying Factors that Buffer Against Decline in Marital Satisfaction after the First Baby Arrives," *Journal of Family Psychology* 14, no. 1 (March 2000): 59–70.

Chapter 6: The Benefits of Supportive Friends

1. Ann L. Dunnewold and Diane G. Sanford, *Life Will Never Be The Same: The Real Mom's Postpartum Survival Guide* (Dallas, Texas: Real Moms Ink LLC, 2010).
2. Ellen Idler, "The Psychological and Physical Benefits of Spiritual/Religious Practices," *Spirituality in Higher Education Newsletter* 4, no. 2 (February 2008).
3. Daniel Goleman, *Social Intelligence: The New Science of Human Relationships* (New York: Bantam Books, 2006).
4. Bert N. Uchino, *Social Support and Physical Health: Understanding the Health Consequences of Relationships* (New Haven, Connecticut: Yale University Press, 2004).
5. Bert N. Uchino, John T. Cacioppo, Janice K. Kiecolt-Glaser, "The Relationship between Social Support and Physiological Processes: A Review with Emphasis on Underlying Mechanisms and Implications for Health," *Psychological Bulletin* 119, no. 3 (May 1996): 488–531.
6. Judith V. Jordan, Alexandra G. Kaplan, Jean Baker Miller, Irene P. Stiver and Janet L. Surrey, *Women's Growth in Connection: Writings from the Stone Center* (New York: The Guilford Press, 1991).
7. Keith Karren, Brent Q. Hafen, Kathryn J. Frandsen and Lee Smith, *Mind/Body Health: The Effects of Attitudes, Emotions, and Relationships*, 4th ed. (San Francisco, California: Benjamin Cummings, 2009).
8. Judith Viorst, "Friends, Good Friends—and Such Good Friends," *Redbook*, 1977.
9. Joyce A. Venis and Suzanne McCloskey, *Postpartum Depression Demystified: An Essential Guide for Understanding and Overcoming the Most Common Complication after Childbirth* (New York: Marlowe & Company, 2007).
10. Karen Kleiman and Valerie Raskin, *This Isn't What I Expected: Overcoming Postpartum Depression* (New York: Bantam Books, 1994).

## *PART III: Principles for Healing, Growing and Finding Meaning from Postpartum Depression*

Chapter 7: Finding Meaning

1. Marianne Williamson, *The Age of Miracles: Embracing the New Midlife* (New York: Hay House, Inc., 2008).

Chapter 8: Principle I: Finding Ways to Heal


1. Lee Lipsenthal, MD, "Mild Depression: Medical Illness or Invitation for Self-Growth?" *Holistic Primary Care* (Spring 2007).
2. Joan Anderson, *The Second Journey: The Road Back to Yourself* (New York: Hyperion, 2008).
3. Kirsten Weir, "The Exercise Effect," *APA Monitor* 42, no. 11 (December 2011).
4. James A. Blumenthal, Michael Babyak, Murali Doraiswamy, MD, Lana Watkins Benson M. Hoffman, Krista A. Barbour, Steve Herman, W. Edward Craighead, Alisha L. Brosse, Robert Waugh, MD, Alan Hinderliter, MD and Andrew Sherwood, "Exercise and Pharmacotherapy in the Treatment of Major Depressive Disorder," *Psychosomatic Medicine* 69, (2007): 587–596.
5. Steven Reinberg, "6 Million U.S. Kids Lack Enough Vitamin D," ABC News, October 2011, http://abcnews.go.com/Health/Healthday/million-us-kids-lack-vitamin/story?id=8917392#.T9YUkbXl-3q.
6. Kinsey Institute, "When the 'Baby Blues' Linger: Investigating Postpartum Depression," *Kinsey Today* (Spring 2009).
7. Mihaly Csikszentmihalyi, "If We Are So Rich, Why Aren't We Happy," *American Psychologist* 54, no. 10 (October 1999).
8. Kelly Lambert, *Lifting Depression: A Neuroscientist's Hands-On Approach to Activating Your Brain's Healing Power* (New York: Basic Books, 2008).
9. EMDR Institute, Inc., "US Basic Training Overview," EMDR Institute, Inc., http://emdr.com/training-information/us-basic-training-overview.html.
10. Mark Sichel, "Music Soothes the Soul," *Psychology Today*, July 15, 2008, http://www.psychologytoday.com/blog/the-therapist-is-in/200807/music-soothes-the-soul.
11. Bridget Grenville-Cleave, "Music and Song: the Sounds of Hope?" *Positive Psychology News Daily*, May 26, 2008, http://positivepsychologynews.com/news/bridget-grenville-cleave/20080526767.
12. Jon Kabat-Zinn, *Wherever You Go, There You Are: Mindfulness Meditation in Everyday Life* (New York: Hyperion, 1994).
13. Ibid.

CHAPTER 10: PRINCIPLE III: THE POWER OF SPIRITUALITY


1. Williamson, *The Age of Miracles.*
2. "Religion," Wikipedia, http://en.wikipedia.org/wiki/Religion.
3. Canadian Counselling and Psychotherapy Association, "Benefits of Faith," *Counselling Connect*, December 22, 2011, http://www.ccpa-accp.ca/blog/?p=1583.
4. Thomas G. Plante, "Religious Faith and Spirituality May Help People Recover from Substance Abuse," American Psychological Association, August 1, 2000, http://www.apa.org/news/press/releases/2000/08/faith.aspx.
5. Keith Karren et al., *Mind/Body Health.*
6. Herbert Benson, *Beyond the Relaxation Response: How to Harness the Healing Power of Your Personal Beliefs* (New York: Berkley Books, 1984).
7. Stephen G. Post, Christina M. Puchalski, MD and David B. Larson, MD, "Physicians and Patient Spirituality: Professional Boundaries, Competency, and Ethics," *Annals of Internal Medicine* 132, no. 7 (April 2000): 578–83.
8. Katherine Kam, "What Is Integrative Medicine?" WebMD, April 16, 2009, http://www.webmd.com/a-to-z-guides/features/alternative-medicine-integrative-medicine.
9. "25 Intriguing Scientific Studies about Faith, Prayer and Healing," Blogging Health Careers, March 31, 2010, http://onlinesurgicaltechniciancourses.com/2010/25-intriguing-scientific-studies-about-faith-prayer-and-healing/.
10. Larry Dossey and David J. Hufford, "Are Prayer Experiments Legitimate? Twenty Criticisms," *Explore* 1, no. 2 (March 2005): 109–117.
11. Robert L. DuPont, MD, "The Healing Power of Faith: Science Explores Medicine's Last Great Frontier," *American Journal of Psychiatry* 158, no. 8 (August 2001): 1347–1348.
12. Idler, "The Psychological and Physical Benefits of Spiritual/Religious Practices."
13. Carl E. Thoresen, "Spirituality and Health: Is There a Relationship?" *Journal of Health Psychology* 4, no. 3 (May 1999): 291–300.
14. Candy Gunther Brown, Stephen C. Mory, MD, Rebecca Williams and Michael J. McClymond, "Study of the Therapeutic Effects of

Proximal Intercessory Prayer (STEPP) on Auditory and Visual Impairments in Rural Mozambique," *Southern Medical Journal* 103, no. 9 (September 2010): 864–869.

15. Betina Yanez, Donald Edmondson, Annette L. Stanton, Crystal L. Park, Lorna Kwan, Patricia A. Ganz and Thomas O. Blank, "Facets of Spirituality as Predictors of Adjustment to Cancer: Relative Contributions of Having Faith and Finding meaning," *Journal of Consulting and Clinical Psychology* 77, no. 4 (August 2009): 730–41.
16. Oprah Winfrey, "What I Know for Sure," *O, the Oprah Magazine*, February 2012.
17. Gabrielle Blair, "I Try to Envision How I Would Be Behaving If I Were Happy," interview by Gretchen Rubin, *The Happiness Project*, February 23, 2012, http://happiness-project.com/happiness_project/2012/02/id-admired-gabrielle-blairs-blog-design-momat-the-intersection-of-design-and-motherhoodfor-a-long-time-clearly-im/.

### Chapter 11: Faith to Get You through Life's Challenges

1. American SIDS Institute, "What is SIDS?" American SIDS Institute, http://sids.org/ndefinition.htm.
2. Lawrence Kushner, *The River of Light: Jewish Mystical Awareness* (Woodstock, Vermont: Jewish Lights Publishing, 2000)

### Chapter 12: Principle IV: The Healing Effect of Your Narrative

1. Jean-Paul Sartre, *Nausea*, trans. Lloyd Alexander (New York: New Directions, 1964).
2. Dan P. McAdams, *The Stories We Live By: Personal Myths and the Making of the Self* (New York: The Guilford Press, 1993).
3. Robert Atkinson, *The Gift of Stories: Practical and Spiritual Applications of Autobiography, Life Stories, and Personal Mythmaking* (Westport, Connecticut: Bergin & Garvey, 1995).